Si King & Dave Myers
THE HAIRY
DIETERS
FAST FOOD

Si King & Dave Myers

THE HAIRY DIETERS

FAST FOOD

We would like to dedicate this book to all the guys and girls, young and old, who've had the spirit to look hard at themselves and give the diet a go. It's not always easy we know, but it's well worth it – and you don't have to starve yourself. We wish you all success, health and happiness. Lots of love Dave and Si xxx

First published in Great Britain in 2016 by
Orion Publishing Group Ltd
Carmelite House
50 Victoria Embankment
London EC4Y 0DZ
An Hachette UK Company

10 9 8 7 6 5 4 3 2

A CIP catalogue record for this book is available from the British Library.

ISBN: 978 0 2976 0931 5

Photographer: Andrew Hayes-Watkins
Food director: Catherine Phipps
Food stylist: Anna Burges-Lumsden
Design and art direction: Abi Hartshorne
Project editor: Jinny Johnson
Prop stylist: Polly Webb-Wilson
Technical artworker: Andy Bowden
Food stylist's assistants: Lou Kenny, Jane Brown
Proofreader: Elise See-Tai
Indexer: Vicki Robinson

Nutritional analysis calculated by:
Fiona Hunter, Bsc (Hons) Nutrition, Dip Dietetics

Printed and bound in Germany

The Orion Publishing Group's policy is to use papers that are natural, renewable and recyclable and made from wood grown in sustainable forests. The logging and manufacturing processes are expected to conform to the environmental regulations of the country of origin.
www.orionbooks.co.uk

Every effort has been made to ensure that the information in this book is accurate. The information will be relevant to the majority of people but may not be applicable in each individual case, so it is advised that professional medical advice is obtained for specific health matters. Neither the publisher, authors or Optomen accept any legal responsibility for any personal injury or other damage or loss arising from the use or misuse of the information in this book. Anyone making a change in their diet should consult their GP, especially if pregnant, infirm, elderly or under 16.

For more delicious recipes, features, videos and exclusives from Orion's cookery writers, and to sign up for our 'Recipe of the Week' email, visit **bybookorbycook.co.uk**

CONTENTS

GOOD FOOD FAST

A few years ago we lost more than six stone between us and we felt fantastic. Since then, cooking from our diet recipes has become a way of life. We've never really gone back to our old ways, but here and there we've gained a bit of weight because of – well, life!

Yes, life. It can get in the way of dieting and all your best intentions, can't it?!

But we've got the answer. We've found that the key to weight loss is to eat good things, fast. If we've got the right food on the table quickly, we don't get tempted by the high-calorie stuff. So we thought if it works for us, it'll work for you too.

This new collection is full of recipes that take just half an hour to prepare and cook. If you've slipped a bit and you've got some timber to shed, the important thing is not to sink into despair and carry on stuffing yourself. Get on to our FAST FOOD plan and you might find you get a nice surprise when you step on the scales one day.

Our food tastes amazing, so non-dieters in the family are happy and you don't suffer while you're losing the pounds. This is real food, not diet food, and once you're at the weight you want to be, our recipes are great for maintaining your figure too.

OUR STORIES

DAVE "Before I started on the diet I was a borderline type-2 diabetic, lining myself up for loads of health problems. Now my sugar levels are normal and have been for the past three years. I have check-ups every six months to make sure I'm on track, and I'm fit and healthy. I'm only human though, and I have a tendency to put on weight so it's a constant battle. And sometimes circumstances make it hard to do what you know you should.

Take last year, for instance. I had a really hectic filming schedule so I was away from home for weeks on end and it was really tough to keep to my normal regime. I did put on a few kilos, but the difference is that now I keep a check on myself and I do something about it. As soon as I was back home and able to cook my own food I lost the weight again, no problem."

SI "I loved being lighter. I'd been a fat lad most of my life and it always got me down. I was one of those people who constantly struggled with my weight, and I wondered why everyone else seemed to be able to eat what they liked and not put on an ounce. Hacked me off right royally to tell the truth.

When finally I had lost weight through working on the Hairy Dieters books and programmes, life intervened with a cruel twist of fate. I found myself seriously ill with a brain aneurysm and I had to fight to get well again. The trauma of all that was incredibly difficult to overcome. I had a prolonged period of inactivity because of the injury to my brain and body, and I found myself not able to do much at all for six months. Making a cup of tea was a big task. Inevitably, with the lack of movement, let alone exercise, I put on weight again.

A year later I looked at myself in the mirror and thought: Oh dear. I really, really have to do something. It took a huge effort but I'm back on track now and losing the weight. I want to be slim again and I'm getting there. And of course, it's great to have the support of my mate Dave. Makes all the difference to have someone to go through it all with, and that's one of the reasons we started the Diet Club. We know that all of you love that support and companionship to help see you through the tricky times."

OUR FAST FOOD CHALLENGE

We're all busy and the problem for many of us is that you get home starving hungry and the temptation is to reach for the snacks or grab a takeaway to fill the gap. So our FAST FOOD challenge was to develop recipes that are quick to make without compromising on taste. Our recipes are just as good as they've always been, but you can have them ready in half an hour so you sit down to your meal before you're tempted to snack. Your hunger is satisfied and you've kept to a reasonable calorie intake. Win, win.

As passionate foodies, our recipes have to be exciting to sustain our interest and we've come up with yet more great ideas to tempt you. Cook these and live like a King – or a Myers – and still lose weight. As always, our recipes are low in calories but high in flavour.

TIPS FOR SPEEDY COOKING

The recipes in this book can be prepped and cooked in about half an hour, but before you start cooking, make sure you have all the ingredients. Our half an hour doesn't include turning out your cupboard to find your curry powder, or running down to the corner shop for an onion. Here are some tips to help you be a super-speedy cook.

- First of all, put a kettle on to boil while you read the recipe through. You're bound to need some hot water and it saves time to pour just-boiled water from a kettle into the saucepan so it comes to the boil more quickly.

- Same with stock. Make sure it's hot before adding it to a dish. If you're using fresh stock, bring it to the boil in a separate pan before using. If using a stock cube or concentrated stock, bring a kettle of water to the boil and use this to make your stock. Adding cold stock will slow down the cooking.

- Simple thing, but when you're bringing something to the boil, put a lid on the pan. It really does make a difference.

- Usually we advise getting all your ingredients chopped and ready before starting to cook, but if you want to have food on the table fast, you might want to get something going while prepping the rest. For example, if a recipe starts with frying an onion, get that in the pan and then chop something else while it's cooking. How do you think a Chinese restaurant gets a banquet ready while you wait?

- As far as possible, make sure meat is at room temperature before you cook it. It cooks quicker that way and it will also be more tender and taste better.

- Be sure your knives are good and sharp – makes chopping and slicing so much faster and easier. Get yourself a good knife sharpener.

SLOW, SLOW, QUICK, QUICK, SLOW

While researching recipes for this book we've discovered the joys of a couple of bits of kit we think you might find useful. Slow cookers and pressure cookers are both tools that can make your diet easier. The idea of a slow cooker might seem a bit odd for a cookbook on fast food, but in fact it can be a brilliant time saver. You just put in your prep time in the morning instead of later and pile all the ingredients into the slow cooker. Then you get home to a beautifully cooked hot meal. What could be better?

Then the pressure cooker – we both remember our mams using pressure cookers and they were scary things, always hissing and exploding. The new ones are very different and perfect for the cook in a hurry. We've found you can make things like a fab risotto, tomato sauce and veggie dhal in a pressure cooker in much less time than usual.

FREEZE IT! ❄

When you're busy and short of time it can be very useful to make double portions of a recipe and freeze some for another day. We've labelled recipes suitable for freezing with the symbol above. Where a recipe contains fresh salad leaves, it's best to freeze the dish without the leaves, then add them after defrosting.

- Wrap food properly in freezer bags or containers and label clearly.
- Never put hot or warm food into the freezer. Always cool food first and preferably chill it in the fridge for a while.
- Freeze food in portions – single portions of things like soup are really useful. If freezing more than one portion, label accordingly.
- Defrost frozen food thoroughly. The safest way is to leave the item in the fridge overnight on a plate to catch any drips. When reheating, make sure the food is piping hot before you eat it.

VEGETARIAN RECIPES V

On some recipes you'll see the symbol above, which means it's suitable for vegetarians as well as non-vegetarians, of course. If you are vegetarian and the recipe contains cheese, make sure the cheese you use doesn't contain animal rennet – some do, some don't, so check the label. One cheese that always contains animal rennet is proper Parmesan, but there are Parmesan-style hard cheeses available, which are fine for vegetarians and will work just as well. For more info on these and other cheeses, have a look at the Vegetarian Society website.

You'll find that you can use lots of the other recipes too by leaving the meat out and using some extra veggies, tofu, soya or Quorn instead. We've worked hard to make sure each recipe has flavour to the max – with or without meat.

HOW TO CHOP AN ONION

You'll find that loads of these recipes start with chopping an onion so it's worth perfecting your technique. That way you'll have a nicely chopped onion and you'll save a few minutes.

1. Trim off the stem end of the onion but leave the root intact.

2. Cut the onion in half, slicing through the root.

3. Peel off the papery skin.

4. Place one half on your chopping board, flat-side down, and hold it firmly in place at the root end. Make a few horizontal cuts into the onion.

5. Then slice down vertically, continuing to hold the onion together at the root end. The more cuts you make, the more finely chopped your onion will be.

6. Now cut across those slices, still holding the onion together at the root end. Repeat with the other half.

HAIRY DIETERS' TIPS

- Don't skip breakfast. You'll only be tempted to stuff yourself mid-morning.

- Eat slowly. Don't gobble your food – chew it well, put your fork down between bites and take your time. Relish every mouthful.

- Before you eat something, ask yourself if you really are hungry. Try having a glass of water – sometimes you're just thirsty, not hungry at all. When you fancy a treat, go sparkling.

- Carry a healthy snack with you when you're out and about. That way you won't be tempted to grab choc bars and crisps. And try taking a flask of soup or a box of home-made salad to work with you for lunch. That way you know exactly what you're eating.

- Don't go shopping for food when you're hungry. You'll be tempted to buy stuff you know you shouldn't be eating.

- Drink water, not sweet fizzy drinks – they're packed with calories. And even innocent-looking drinks like fresh juices and smoothies are high calorie and best avoided. Cut down on alcohol too.

- Use smaller plates and take smaller portions. We were always generous with our helpings before, but now we stick to sensible portions. Don't guess – use your kitchen scales.

- Trim visible fat off meat, or buy leaner cuts. Loin means lean. Belly pork is great but not for your belly.

- If you do fancy some French bread, take out some of the stodge and just enjoy the crunchy crust. This goes for bread rolls too.

- When you feel like you want another helping, wait 20 minutes. It takes that long for the message that you're full to get through to your brain and you'll probably find you don't need any more food after all.

- Look out for hidden sugar in foods such as ready meals and fruity yoghurts. It's surprising how much there is and it ups the calorie count.

- Weigh yourself regularly but be prepared for little variations. Some people like to get on the scales every day, while others prefer once or twice a week, but the important thing is to keep a check on yourself.

- Don't pick as you cook. Dave's mam said, "Folks who are pickers need bigger knickers!"

FEEDING FRIENDS

When you've got friends and family coming round it's tempting to have a night off the diet, but with our recipes there's no need. You can make a delicious meal without breaking your calorie limits, allowing you to stick to your diet and do your guests' waistlines a favour too. Don't tell them that the food is low calorie. They'll never guess and they'll just think you're an amazingly talented cook!

Here are couple of ideas for menus from this book:

MENU 1

Wild mushroom soup
(74 calories per serving)

Fish Véronique
(231 calories per serving)

Raspberry and
orange soufflés
(105 calories per serving)

Add some veg or salad and
you have a three-course meal
for around 500 calories

MENU 2

Spicy mussels
(160 calories per serving)

Pork and black
bean stew
(380 calories per serving)

Instant sorbet
(87 calories per serving)

Three really great courses for
just over 600 calories

MENU 3

And if you feel like treating
yourself to one of our more
lavish puds, go for a low-cal
main course first

Mediterranean fish soup
(220 calories per serving)

Quick rice pudding
with marsala sauce
(341 calories per serving)

A FEW LITTLE NOTES FROM US

- We've given calorie counts for our dishes so follow the recipe carefully so you don't change the count. Weigh ingredients and use proper spoons and a measuring jug. We always say how many people a recipe serves, so you don't eat more than your share.

- We mention spray oil in quite a few recipes, as this is an easy way of reducing the amount of oil you use. Buy the most natural kind you can find and spritz it lightly. If you don't want to use spray oil, just brush on a small amount of oil with a pastry brush.

- Peel onions, garlic and all other vegetables and fruit unless otherwise specified.

- Use free-range eggs and free-range chicken whenever possible. Whatever you're cooking, it always pays to buy the best and freshest seasonal ingredients you can afford. We reckon that 95 per cent of good cooking is good shopping – great ingredients need less fussing with.

- If you're really organised you might have some of your own home-made stock in your freezer. Otherwise, it's fine to use the fresh stocks available in the supermarkets or buy cubes or the little stockpots. Many are pretty good these days.

BREAKFAST AND BRUNCH

BIKER BREAKFAST MUFFINS

MASALA OMELETTE

MENEMEN (TURKISH EGGS)

FRENCH TOAST

SMOOTHIES

BREAKFAST CRANACHAN

STOVE-TOP GRANOLA

CAULIFLOWER RICE KEDGEREE

CORNED BEEF HASH

BIKER BREAKFAST MUFFINS

We reinvented the doner kebab and now it's the turn of the breakfast muffin – this is our guilty secret that isn't a secret any more. Okay, they're 500 calories but let's call them brunch and enjoy. The sausages lose a lot of fat when they're cooked in this way so that cuts the calories, or you could try making the chicken/turkey patties instead, which are definitely much lower cal. We love fried eggs and they're quicker than poached so extra good when you're in a rush.

Put a griddle pan over a high heat and leave it to get really hot – at least 5 minutes. If using sausages, remove the skins and shape each one into a very flat, round patty.

If you want to make the chicken or turkey patties instead of using sausages, put the mince in a bowl. Trim the bacon of fat and dice it as finely as you can, then add it to the bowl with the sage and the tomato purée. Season well with salt and lots of black pepper. Form the mixture into 4 patties.

When the griddle is too hot to hold your hand over, add whichever patties you've made. Grill them for 3 minutes on each side, adding a cheese slice, if using, to each for the last minute. If the griddle pan is hot enough, the patties will not stick.

Spray a large frying pan with low-cal oil. Break the eggs into the pan and cook them over a medium heat until the whites are just set.

Meanwhile, split and toast the muffins. Add a patty to 4 of the muffin halves. If you have time, trim the eggs for neatness and place an egg on top of each patty. Top with the remaining muffin halves and serve immediately. If you want to reduce the calorie count a little, leave off the top muffin.

SERVES 4

4 high-meat content sausages (about 65g each)

4 slices of reduced-fat cheese (optional)

low-cal oil spray

4 eggs

4 muffins

Chicken or turkey patties (optional)

250g lean turkey or chicken mince

1 rasher of smoked back bacon

1 tsp dried sage

1 tbsp tomato purée

flaked sea salt

freshly ground black pepper

500 calories per serving (fully loaded with cheese and muffin top and bottom)
444 calories per serving (as above, but with chicken or turkey patties)

MASALA OMELETTE

If you're the sort of person who often craves a curry, try this indulgent breakfast. It's a perfect example of our mantra – there are no calories in flavour. This is a great spicy kick-start of a dish and once you've got the spices out of the cupboard it's ready in no time.

SERVES 2

1 tsp coconut or vegetable oil
1 small onion, finely chopped
1 chilli, finely chopped
1 garlic clove, finely chopped
5g fresh root ginger, grated
½ tsp nigella seeds (optional)
1 tsp ground cumin
½ tsp ground turmeric
pinch of cinnamon
4 eggs, beaten
a few coriander leaves
flaked sea salt
freshly ground black pepper

Heat the oil in a large frying pan. Add the onion and cook it over a medium heat for about 5 minutes until it's just starting to colour. It's nice if the onion has a bit of bite to it so don't worry if it's not really soft.

Add the chilli (deseeded if you want), garlic, grated ginger and nigella seeds, if using. Sprinkle in the spices, then stir for a couple more minutes.

Season the eggs with salt and pepper. Pour the eggs into the frying pan and swirl the mixture around to make sure it covers the base of the pan evenly. Cook for a few minutes until the eggs are just set. Sprinkle with coriander leaves, roll the omelette up or cut it in half and divide it between 2 plates.

V

190 calories per serving

MENEMEN (TURKISH EGGS)

You get some fab breakfasts in Turkey and this is one of our favourites. It's so good you might find you like it better than a full English and the bonus is it's low in calories. We like to crumble in some feta when serving but it does add a few cals – up to you.

SERVES 4

1 tbsp olive oil

1 small red onion, finely chopped

1 red pepper, deseeded and diced

1 green pepper, finely diced

1 tsp hot smoked paprika or chilli powder

1 tsp dried oregano

1 tbsp tomato purée

4 medium tomatoes, diced or 200g canned chopped tomatoes

8 eggs, beaten

flaked sea salt

freshly ground black pepper

To serve

50g feta, crumbled (optional)

parsley or mint leaves, finely chopped

Heat the olive oil in a large frying pan that has a lid. Add the onion and peppers and cook them over a medium heat for about 10 minutes, covered, stirring regularly. They should still have some texture – you don't want them to be very soft.

Sprinkle over the paprika or chilli powder and the oregano. Add the tomato purée and cook for a further couple of minutes, then add the tomatoes and simmer for 5 minutes.

Season the eggs with salt and black pepper. Add them to the tomatoes and cook, stirring constantly, uncovered, until the eggs have completely combined with the tomato mixture and are just cooked through – the consistency should be soft. Serve immediately, sprinkled with feta, if using, and parsley or mint leaves.

Biker tip: If you're vegetarian, make sure the feta cheese you use is suitable and doesn't contain animal rennet.

V

231 calories per serving
264 calories per serving with feta

FRENCH TOAST

We both love French toast for a really indulgent breakfast treat – but it doesn't love our waistlines. So we've come up with a clever new version that cuts the fat right back and adds sweetness with a lovely apple compote. You could pop a few blackberries into the compote if you like or just scatter some on the plate. Lip-smackingly good.

First make the compote. Put the diced apples in a saucepan, squeeze the lemon juice over them and add 100ml of water. Simmer the apples over a low heat until they have softened and broken down – this only takes 5 minutes or so. Sprinkle in the cinnamon and pour over the maple syrup, then stir to combine. It's fine for the compote to be quite lumpy.

While the apples are cooking, get everything ready for the French toast. Break the eggs into a large bowl and add the milk, sugar and cinnamon. Whisk thoroughly until the eggs are completely broken up and combined with the other ingredients.

Heat a large frying pan and grease it with low-cal oil spray. Lightly wipe the pan over with kitchen towel to make sure the spray covers the base evenly. Press each slice of bread into the milk and egg mixture until it has just soaked through – don't let the bread become saturated or it will be in danger of falling apart. Shake off any excess and immediately drop the bread on to the frying pan and repeat with the other slices. Cook for a couple of minutes on each side until heated through and well browned on both sides.

Serve the French toast with the apple compote, a few blackberries, if you like, and a dollop of low-fat Greek yoghurt or crème fraiche.

SERVES 4

2 large eggs

200ml whole milk

1 tsp sugar

½ tsp cinnamon

low-cal oil spray

4 fairly thick slices of bread

Apple compote

2 large Bramley apples (about 300g peeled weight), peeled and diced

squeeze of lemon juice

½ tsp cinnamon

2 tbsp maple syrup

To serve

blackberries (optional)

low-fat Greek yoghurt or crème fraiche

281 calories per serving

SMOOTHIES

You can't say us Bikers don't move with the times – we're well up with smoothies. These make a proper get-up-and-go breakfast and you can take them to work with you if you like.

APPLE AND OAT SMOOTHIE

SERVES 2

2 eating apples, cored and roughly chopped

squeeze of lemon juice

2 tbsp porridge oats

200ml fat-free yoghurt

300ml semi-skimmed milk

½ tsp cinnamon

1 tsp honey

Put the chopped apples in a blender and squeeze the lemon juice over them. Add all the remaining ingredients and blitz until the mixture is as smooth as you can get it. Divide it between 2 glasses and serve at once.

V   *275 calories per serving*

AVOCADO, GRAPE AND SPINACH SMOOTHIE

SERVES 2

1 avocado

1 pear, roughly chopped

150g green grapes

handful of spinach

juice of 1 lime

handful of ice cubes

Peel the avocado and remove the stone. Put the avocado flesh in a blender with the rest of the ingredients and blitz until beautifully smooth. If the smoothie is too thick for your taste, add a little water to make the consistency you like. Divide between 2 glasses and serve at once.

V   *244 calories per serving*

BREAKFAST CRANACHAN

Breakfast doesn't get easier than this. Oats are a staple for us in the morning and this is a good twist on a bowl of porridge. Great for breakfast but can also be enjoyed of an evening with a tot of whisky if you want to treat yourself.

SERVES 4

40g porridge oats

200g raspberries and/or blueberries

400g low-fat or 0%-fat yoghurt

4 tsp honey

V   *134 calories per serving*

Put the porridge oats in a frying pan. Toast them over a high heat, stirring or shaking them regularly, until they smell nutty and have started to turn a light golden brown. Remove the pan from the heat, tip the oats on to a plate and leave them to cool for a couple of minutes.

Layer the berries, yoghurt and oats in individual glasses and drizzle a teaspoon of honey over each. Gently stir the mixture to get a nice ripple effect, then serve immediately before the oats go soft.

STOVE-TOP GRANOLA

When we first started dieting it was a real shock to find out that what we thought was a healthy granola breakfast actually had twice the calories of a fry-up. Best thing is to make your own granola and this version is cooked in a frying pan and takes minutes to put together. We think jumbo oats work best, as they give a chunkier texture.

SERVES 6

2 tbsp maple syrup

20g butter or coconut oil

150g jumbo oats

pinch of salt

1 tbsp sunflower seeds

2 tbsp flaked almonds

50g dried fruit

V *213 calories per serving (without milk or yoghurt)*

Put the maple syrup and the butter or coconut oil in a large, preferably non-stick, frying pan and melt them together over a low heat.

Add the jumbo oats with a pinch of salt. Stir until the oats are completely coated with the melted syrup and butter, then turn up the heat to medium. Spread the oats evenly over the base of the pan, leave them for about 20 seconds, then stir and repeat. Keep doing this until all the oats have turned a golden brown and smell nutty – this will take about 5 minutes.

Add the sunflower seeds, nuts and fruit and stir for a couple of minutes longer. Tip the granola on to a plate and let it cool for 5 minutes – the oats will crisp up more. Serve at once with milk or yoghurt and store any leftovers in an airtight container for another day.

CAULIFLOWER RICE KEDGEREE

We're huge fans of cauli rice and cauliflower goes well with curry. Put them together and you've got kedgeree, which has always been a favourite of ours. Clever eh? This makes a cracking supper dish as well as a good way to start the day.

SERVES 4

4 eggs

500g cauliflower

500g smoked haddock, skinned

250ml whole milk

1 tsp coconut oil or vegetable oil

small bunch of spring onions, finely sliced into rounds

1 garlic clove, crushed

5g fresh root ginger, finely chopped

1 tbsp mild curry powder

150g frozen peas

small bunch of coriander (optional)

312 calories per serving

Boil a full kettle of water. Pour some just-boiled water into a small saucepan and bring it back to the boil. Add the eggs and boil them for 6 minutes. Remove the pan from the heat and run the eggs under cold water to cool them down.

While the eggs are cooking, divide the cauliflower into florets and put them, stalks and all, into a food processor. Blitz them to the texture of fine breadcrumbs.

Place the haddock in a shallow pan that has a lid and pour over the milk, then place the pan over a medium heat. Top up with just-boiled water from the kettle so the haddock is just covered, then bring the liquid back to the boil. Put a lid on the pan, remove it from the heat and leave it to stand for 10 minutes.

Melt the oil in a large frying pan over a gentle heat and add the spring onions. Cook them for a couple of minutes, then add the garlic, ginger and curry powder. Cook for a further minute.

Add the cauliflower to the frying pan and about 100ml of the haddock poaching liquid. Cook, stirring regularly, for about 5 minutes until the water has been absorbed and the cauliflower looks dry and fluffy.

Put the peas in the small saucepan and pour over some just-boiled water. Place the pan over the heat, bring the water back the boil and cook the peas for a couple of minutes. Drain and add the peas to the cauliflower.

Remove the haddock from its poaching liquid and break it up into small chunks, discarding any bones you may find. Peel the eggs and cut them into quarters.

Gently stir the haddock into the cauliflower rice, then top with the eggs and some coriander leaves if you like.

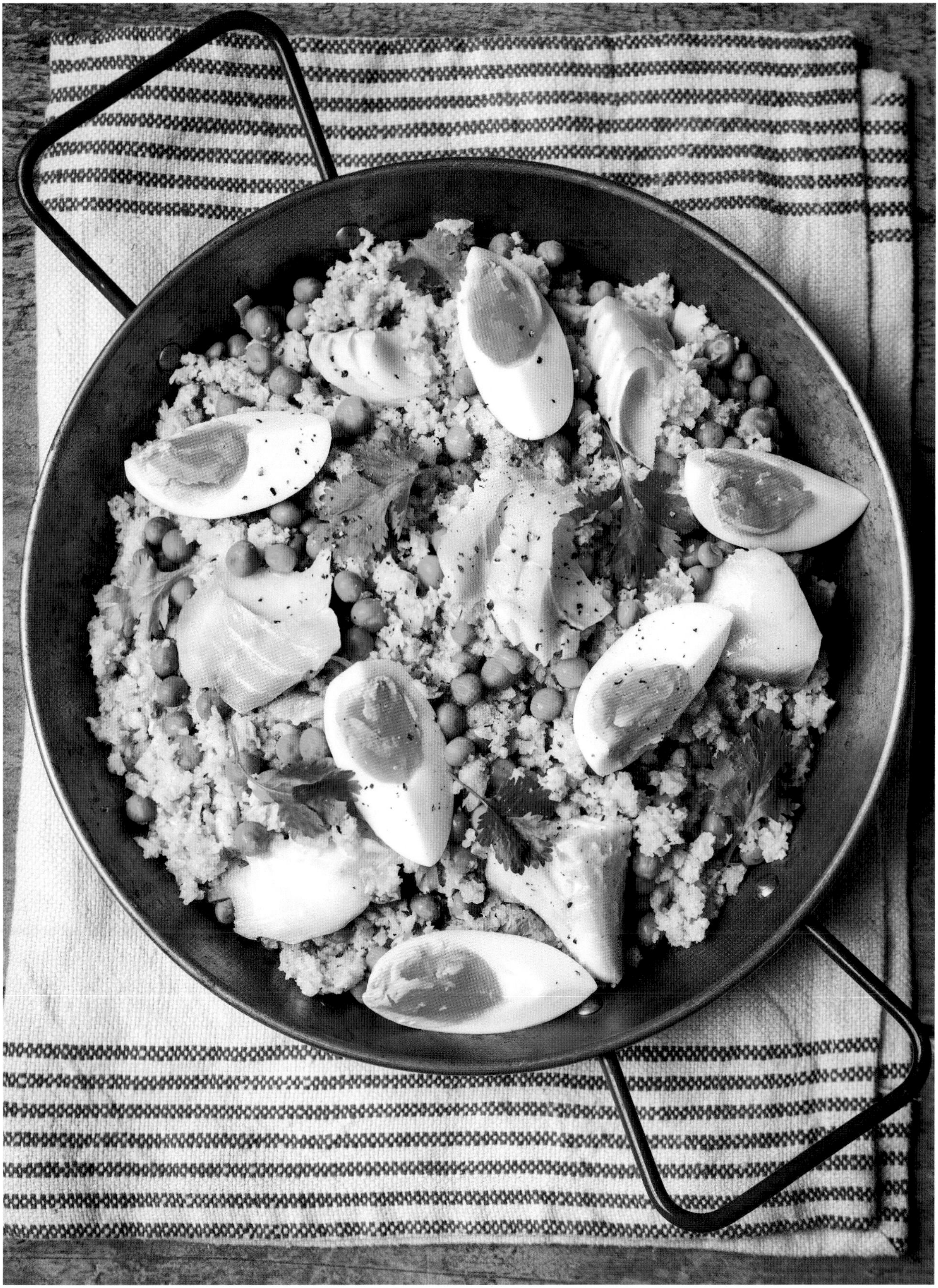

CORNED BEEF HASH

This is a proper feast of a breakfast and by using carrot and celeriac instead of potato, you cut calories and add flavour. We usually make this with a can of corned beef, which is good stuff, but we've also tried it with leftover home-made corned beef and it's even better. There's a recipe in our Meat Feasts *book if you want to try it. It's not as fatty as the tinned beef either.*

SERVES 4

200g celeriac, finely diced

200g carrots, finely diced

1 tsp dripping or fat scraped from the corned beef

1 onion, finely chopped

1 tbsp tomato purée

1 tsp Dijon mustard

200g can of corned beef or equivalent, diced

100ml beef stock

1 tsp Worcestershire sauce

low-cal oil spray

4 eggs

248 calories per serving

Bring a kettle of water to the boil while you prepare the celeriac and carrots. Put the veg in a saucepan and pour over just-boiled water to cover. Bring the water back to the boil, cover the pan and cook the vegetables for 7 minutes. They should be just cooked through. Drain thoroughly.

Meanwhile, heat the fat in a large frying pan. Add the onion and cook it over a medium heat until it's starting to soften. As soon as the vegetables are ready, add them to the frying pan along with the corned beef. Cook for 5 minutes until a crust has formed on the bottom of the mixture.

Put the tomato purée and mustard into a small bowl or jug with the beef stock and Worcestershire sauce and whisk well. Pour this mixture over the corned beef and vegetables and stir thoroughly. Cook for another 10 minutes, stirring every so often, until there are plenty of crusty brown bits interspersed through the mix.

While the hash finishes cooking, heat another frying pan and spray it with oil. Add the eggs and fry them until the whites have just set. Serve the hash with the eggs on top.

SOUPS AND STARTERS

PEA, LETTUCE AND ASPARAGUS SOUP

SPICY SWEETCORN SOUP

WILD MUSHROOM SOUP

CHILL-OUT SOUP

MEDITERRANEAN FISH SOUP

RED LENTIL AND BACON SOUP

BIKER CHICKEN SOUP

SPICY MUSSELS

AMERICAN-STYLE PRAWN COCKTAIL

SALT AND PEPPER SQUID

SALMON CEVICHE

PEA, LETTUCE AND ASPARAGUS SOUP

Get your fill of chlorophyll – this soup makes you feel healthy just looking at it. It's an ideal quick meal and the short cooking time keeps the lovely fresh green colour.

SERVES 4

10g butter
1 leek, trimmed and finely diced
100g thin asparagus spears
2 little gem lettuces, shredded
600g frozen peas or petits pois
1 litre hot vegetable stock
squeeze of lemon or lime juice
flaked sea salt
freshly ground black pepper

To serve

2 tbsp single cream
small bunch of basil or mint

V ❄ *220 calories per serving*

Heat the butter in a large saucepan. Add the diced leek and a splash of water, then put a lid on the pan and leave it over a low heat for 5 minutes.

Cut the tips off the asparagus and set them aside for later. Finely slice the remaining stems and add these to the leeks, along with the shredded lettuce. Cook for another couple of minutes, then add the peas and pour the hot stock into the pan. Season with salt and pepper and leave the soup to simmer for 5 minutes.

While the soup is simmering, heat a griddle until it's very hot and grill the asparagus tips until they're nicely charred.

Blend the soup to a smooth texture. Taste, then squeeze in a little lemon or lime juice – just enough to bring out the flavour. If you have a mini blender or food processor, blitz the cream with the basil or mint, but if not, just finely chop the herbs and stir them into the cream.

Serve the soup drizzled with a little of the herb cream and topped with the grilled asparagus.

SPICY SWEETCORN SOUP

You know we like a bit of spice and heat, and this soup really does the trick. It's got a bacon garnish as well, but still comes in at only 274 calories a bowlful. Top that! Take a flaskful of this to work with you to keep your spirits up.

SERVES 4

2 tsp vegetable oil

1 small onion, finely chopped

1 red pepper, deseeded and diced

1 garlic clove, finely chopped

1 sweet potato, finely diced

3 tsp chipotle paste

1 tsp ground cumin

bunch of coriander, stems and leaves separated and chopped

700g frozen sweetcorn

400g can of chopped tomatoes

1 litre hot chicken or vegetable stock

75g smoked back bacon, trimmed of fat and cut into fine strips

flaked sea salt

freshly ground black pepper

❄ *274 calories per serving*

Heat 1 teaspoon of the oil in a large saucepan. Add the onion and pepper and fry them gently for a few minutes, stirring regularly, then add the garlic and sweet potato. Stir for a minute.

Add 2 teaspoons of the chipotle paste and the cumin and stir to coat the vegetables. Add the chopped coriander stems and sweetcorn, then pour in the tomatoes and stock. Season with salt and pepper.

Bring the soup to the boil, then turn the heat down and simmer for 10 minutes, until the sweet potato is tender.

Meanwhile, heat the remaining oil in a small frying pan and fry the bacon for a couple of minutes. Add the rest of the chipotle paste and stir until the bacon is coated in the chipotle.

Ladle half the soup into a blender and blitz it to a purée, then tip it back into the saucepan with the rest. Alternatively, use a stick blender to whizz the soup so it thickens but still has some texture.

Serve in deep bowls garnished with the chipotle bacon and some coriander leaves.

Biker tip: For a vegetarian version, use veggie stock and garnish the soup with smoked tofu instead of bacon. Buy the firm tofu so you can crisp it up nicely before adding it to the soup.

WILD MUSHROOM SOUP

This is a beautifully rich and tasty soup with a proper mushroomy aroma. It's a soup for the gourmet and ideal for serving up to guests – no one will guess it's so low in calories. You don't have to use wild mushrooms; portobello, chestnut or button are fine, or try a mixture of them all. You could add a swirl of oil or crème fraiche to each serving if you're feeling fancy.

SERVES 4

20g dried wild or porcini mushrooms

150ml just-boiled water

10g butter

2 shallots or 1 leek, finely chopped

1 garlic clove, finely chopped

500g fresh mushrooms, wiped clean and sliced

700ml hot vegetable stock

a large sprig of thyme

25ml sherry or Marsala or juice of ½ lemon

2 tbsp finely chopped parsley

flaked sea salt

freshly ground black pepper

Put the dried mushrooms in a bowl. Pour the just-boiled water over them and leave them to soak for 10 minutes while you get on with the rest of the preparations.

Heat the butter in a heavy-based saucepan. Add the shallots or leek to the pan, put the lid on and leave to cook over a low heat for 5 minutes. Add the garlic and fresh mushrooms, turn up the heat and cook for a couple of minutes.

Strain the soaked mushrooms, reserving the liquid, then chop them finely and add them to the pan. Pour in the reserved liquid and the hot stock, then add the thyme and season with salt and pepper.

Bring the soup to the boil and simmer it for 5 minutes. Add the sherry, Marsala or lemon juice, remove the sprig of thyme, then blitz the soup in a blender. It should be a lovely rich brown. Serve immediately with a sprinkling of parsley.

V ❄ *74 calories per serving*

CHILL-OUT SOUP

This is a soup that thinks it's a smoothie and since there's no cooking needed it's super-quick to put together – perfect for a refreshing snack. For best results, keep the melon and cucumber in the fridge until you're ready to make the soup, although you can always add ice cubes if necessary. The garlic does add a nice savoury depth to the flavour, but if you're not a garlic fan, leave it out. We advise using green melon such as honeydew or Galia, as the orange ones, like cantaloupe, make a rather beige soup, which is less appealing.

Peel and deseed the melon and cut the flesh into chunks. Peel the whole cucumber and cut it into chunks too, then put both in a blender and blitz briefly.

Cut the remaining unpeeled cucumber into chunks and add these to the blender with the ginger, chilli, garlic, if using, lime juice, vinegar and plenty of salt and pepper. Blitz again, but stop when the mixture has fine flecks of chilli and unpeeled cucumber. You don't want a completely smooth texture.

Mix the herbs with the olive oil – you can do this in a small blender or food processor. Pour the soup into bowls and top with a swirl of yoghurt and a few drops of the herb oil. Serve with lime wedges on the side to squeeze over if you like.

SERVES 4

½ large honeydew or Galia melon, well chilled

1½ large cucumbers, well chilled

7g fresh root ginger, grated

1 red or green chilli, deseeded and finely chopped

1 garlic clove, grated (optional)

juice of 2 limes

½ tsp white wine vinegar

flaked sea salt

freshly ground black pepper

To serve

small bunch of mint, coriander or basil, finely chopped

1 tbsp olive oil

100ml yoghurt or crème fraiche

lime wedges (optional)

106 calories per serving

V

MEDITERRANEAN FISH SOUP

This might look like a lot to do in half an hour, but it's really just a bit of chopping and then chucking it all in the pan. Very little cooking needed. The rouille is optional but really does add great flavour – rouille is the traditional accompaniment to Mediterranean fish soup and is served alongside for everyone to stir in as they like. It's usually made with shedloads of olive oil but our cheat's version is much lower in calories and still tastes the business.

If you're making the rouille, it's probably best to do this first and leave it to stand while you're preparing the soup. Put the saffron with a tablespoon of hot water in a small bowl. Add the mayonnaise and red peppers to a food processor with the lemon juice, then crush the garlic into this mixture and add the cayenne and the saffron water. Season with salt and pepper and blitz until smooth. Tip the rouille into a bowl, cover and set aside until needed.

Put the saffron for the soup in a small bowl with a tablespoon of hot water and leave it to steep while you prepare the vegetables.

Heat the olive oil and butter in a large saucepan or a casserole dish with a lid. Add the onion, garlic, leek and fennel and stir to coat them with the oil and butter, then add the whole chilli. Pour in the white wine and put the lid on the pan. Leave to cook gently over a low heat for 5 minutes.

Add the fish stock, orange peel, bay leaf and the saffron and its liquid. Season with salt and pepper, then bring the soup to the boil and leave it to simmer for a further 5 minutes. Add the courgette to the soup and cook for a further 3 minutes while you dice the fish.

Turn up the heat and add the fish and prawns, then the Ouzo or Pernod, if using. Put the lid on the pan and cook for 5–10 minutes or until the fish and prawns are cooked through. Sprinkle with parsley and serve with the rouille, if you've made some, on the side.

SERVES 4

pinch of saffron strands

1 tsp olive oil

5g butter

1 onion, finely chopped

3 garlic cloves, finely chopped

1 leek, trimmed and thinly sliced

1 fennel bulb, trimmed and thinly sliced

1 red chilli (optional)

100ml white wine

1 litre hot fish stock

1 strip of thinly pared orange peel

1 bay leaf

1 courgette, diced

500g white fish fillets, skinned

12 raw tiger prawns, peeled

1 tsp Ouzo or Pernod (optional)

2 tbsp finely chopped parsley

flaked sea salt

freshly ground black pepper

Rouille (optional)

small pinch of saffron

2 tbsp low-cal mayonnaise

2 roasted red peppers (from a jar)

juice of ½ lemon

1 garlic clove

pinch of cayenne

220 calories per serving

RED LENTIL AND BACON SOUP

This is a proper pick-me-up of a soup – comforting and rich in protein with the lentils. Red lentils cook quickly and break down nicely so you can make a good soup in a short time. Be sure to add hot stock though, or the cooking time will be longer. We like the chunky texture of this soup, but you can blend it if you like.

Heat the oil in a large saucepan and add the bacon, onion and red pepper. Cook over a low heat for 5 minutes, until the vegetables have started to soften.

Add the sweet potato, garlic and lentils to the pan and stir for a minute. Pour the hot stock into the pan, add the herbs and season with salt and pepper. Quickly bring the soup back to the boil over a high heat, then turn the heat down to medium and cover the pan. Cook for 15–20 minutes until the red lentils are tender. Take out the herbs before serving.

SERVES 4

1 tsp olive oil

75g smoked back bacon, trimmed of fat and diced

1 onion, finely chopped

1 red pepper, deseeded and diced

1.5 litres hot chicken or vegetable stock

1 small sweet potato, finely diced

1 garlic clove, finely chopped

200g red lentils

large sprig of thyme

1 bay leaf

flaked sea salt

freshly ground black pepper

321 calories per serving

BIKER CHICKEN SOUP

This is a meal in a bowl and even with a hunk of bread you come in at under 500 cals. It's what you bought that food flask for and is ideal for taking to work. We use cooked chicken breasts – available in every supermarket – for our quick version and it's a real feast. The tarragon is optional but it does add a lovely bit of extra flavour so pop some in if you can.

SERVES 4

1 onion, finely diced

1 large carrot, finely diced

1 celery stick, finely diced

150g butternut squash (peeled weight)

150g celeriac (peeled weight)

1 medium potato (about 150g), finely diced

2 leeks, cut into thin rounds

1 tbsp olive oil

50g smoked back bacon, trimmed of fat and diced

1 litre hot chicken stock

1 tsp dried oregano

1 bay leaf

1 sprig of tarragon (optional)

1 small green cabbage or a small bunch of kale or cavolo nero, finely shredded

2 cooked chicken breasts, finely shredded

small bunch of parsley, chopped

squeeze of lemon (optional)

flaked sea salt

freshly ground black pepper

Prepare the onion, carrot, celery, squash, celeriac, potato and leeks.

Heat the olive oil in a large saucepan, add the bacon and cook it over a high heat for a couple of minutes. Add the vegetables and cook them over a medium heat for 5 minutes, until they start to take on a little colour.

Pour the hot chicken stock into the pan and add the herbs, including the tarragon, if using. Season the soup with salt and pepper, bring it to the boil and then turn down the heat so it's cooking somewhere between a simmer and a proper rolling boil. Partially cover with a lid and leave for 5 minutes.

Meanwhile, prepare the cabbage, kale or cavolo nero and the chicken, add them to the pan and continue to cook for a further 10 minutes. By this point all the vegetables should be cooked through and the potato should have broken down a little.

Stir in most of the parsley, leaving a few leaves to garnish each serving. Taste and add a squeeze of lemon juice if you think the soup needs it.

363 calories per serving

SPICY MUSSELS

Mussels are cheap, tasty and nutritious. Eat more of them and you'll soon lose your belly and see your muscles! This spicy dish makes a good light meal on its own, perhaps with a bit of bread to mop up the delicious juices, but you can make it more substantial if you like by adding some canned cannellini beans. If you want to do this, add the beans with the passata and don't forget to tot up the calories too.

SERVES 4

1 tbsp olive oil

50g smoked back bacon, trimmed of fat and diced

1 onion, thinly sliced

2 garlic cloves, finely chopped

1 tsp fennel seeds

1 tsp hot paprika

grated zest of 1 lemon

100ml red wine

200ml tomato passata

1kg mussels

handful of parsley, finely chopped

flaked sea salt

freshly ground black pepper

160 calories per serving

Heat the olive oil in a heavy-based saucepan, then add the bacon and fry until it's crisp and brown. Remove it with a slotted spoon and set aside.

Add the onion to the pan and cook it gently for several minutes until it's starting to soften, then add the garlic, fennel seeds, paprika and lemon zest. Pour the red wine into the pan and let it bubble up for a minute or so, then add the passata. Turn the heat down to a simmer and put a lid on the pan. Leave for another 5 minutes.

While the sauce is simmering, clean the mussels under cold running water and pull off any beards. Tap any open shells and throw away any mussels that don't close tightly.

Add the mussels to the pan and put the lid back on. Cook for 3–4 minutes, shaking the pan regularly until the mussels have cooked through and have opened fully.

Sprinkle the bacon and parsley over the mussels. Check the seasoning and add salt and pepper if needed. Serve immediately, discarding any mussels that remain closed.

AMERICAN-STYLE PRAWN COCKTAIL

*If you're in a big rush you can use ready-cooked prawns for this, but if you can spend
a few minutes giving some raw prawns a spicy rub before whacking them on to a hot griddle
you'll have something really special. Quick to do and so good to eat. The only problem is that it's
so moreish you might be tempted to eat it all.*

SERVES 4

20 raw large peeled prawns,
tail tips attached if possible

1 tsp flaked sea salt

½ tsp white peppercorns

1 tsp garlic powder

grated zest of 1 lemon

1 tbsp olive oil

lemon wedges, to serve

Sauce

2 tbsp tomato ketchup

2 tbsp hot horseradish sauce

juice of 1 lemon

dash of Tabasco sauce

dash of Worcestershire sauce

pinch of paprika (optional)

flaked sea salt

freshly ground black pepper

103 calories per serving

Heat a griddle pan for a few minutes until it's very hot. Check the
prawns and remove the black line running down the back – this is
the intestinal tract. Put the prawns in a bowl.

Grind the salt, peppercorns, garlic powder and lemon zest together
with a pestle and mortar, then stir in the olive oil. Add the mixture
to the bowl with the prawns and rub it into them, making sure
they are all well coated.

Cook the prawns on the hot griddle for a minute or so on each side
until they're pink and just cooked through.

For the sauce, mix together all the ingredients (except the paprika
and seasoning) in a small bowl. Season with salt and pepper and
sprinkle with a little paprika if you like. Serve the prawns with
the sauce for dipping, with extra lemon wedges for squeezing
over the top.

SALT AND PEPPER SQUID

Deep-fried squid is good but so is this griddled version – and it's far lower in calories. You can buy cleaned squid at fish counters so all you need to do is open out the tubes and score them as we describe below. If the tentacles are included, cook them too. Enjoy with a dash of Tabasco.

Place a griddle pan over a high heat for at least 5 minutes, while you get the squid ready.

Take each squid pouch or tube and pull off the fins if they're still attached. Slide your knife inside the top opening of the pouch, then cut down the side, so you can open the squid out into a flat piece. Lie the piece outer side down and lightly cut a diagonal pattern over the inner side with a sharp knife, making sure that you don't cut right the way through. Do the same with the fins. Cut the tubes into strips 2cm wide.

Crush the black peppercorns, mix them with the sea salt and lemon zest and sprinkle the mixture over the squid – tentacles too, if you have them. Drizzle over the olive oil.

Cook the squid on the hot griddle for 1–2 minutes on each side until nicely charred – the pieces of squid will curl round on themselves, which is fine. You may have to cook the squid in a couple of batches so you don't overcrowd the griddle. If so, make sure the griddle is still very hot when you start the second batch.

Serve the squid piping hot, with a squeeze of lemon juice and a dash of Tabasco, if you like. Or if you want some extra zing, sprinkle the squid with Szechuan peppercorns – half a teaspoon should do it.

SERVES 4

500g small squid, cleaned
1 tsp black peppercorns
1 tsp crushed sea salt
grated zest of 1 lemon
1 tbsp olive oil

To serve
lemon wedges
Tabasco sauce (optional)
½ tsp Szechuan peppercorns

121 calories per serving

SALMON CEVICHE

Ceviche is a Peruvian favourite – it's really just thinly sliced raw fish served in citrus juices and other flavourings. The marinade 'cooks' the fish so it has a lovely texture but still tastes really fresh. This makes a perfect starter or a light lunch.

SERVES 4

400g salmon fillet

2 spring onions

4 radishes

1 tbsp finely shredded
coriander leaves

1 tbsp finely shredded
basil leaves

Dressing

juice of 2 limes

juice of 1 orange

1 garlic clove, finely chopped

5g fresh root ginger,
finely chopped

1 red chilli, finely chopped

1 tbsp finely chopped
coriander stems

flaked sea salt

freshly ground black pepper

First make the dressing. Mix the lime and orange juice in a bowl and add the garlic, ginger, red chilli and coriander stems. Season with salt and pepper, then leave the dressing to stand for 5 minutes while you prepare the fish and vegetables.

Using a sharp, long-bladed knife, carefully slice the salmon as thinly as you can. Start with the knife just under the surface and cut very thin slices on the diagonal towards the tip of the fillet, as you would for smoked salmon. Discard the skin. Arrange the slices on 4 plates.

Cut each spring onion in half, lengthways, then shred finely. Cut the radishes into thin slices and sprinkle them over the salmon.

Finally, drizzle the dressing over the salmon – it should be well covered – then sprinkle with shredded coriander and basil leaves. Serve immediately.

229 calories per serving

SALADS AND SAVOURY SNACKS

HARISSA VEGETABLES AND JUMBO COUSCOUS

SEVEN-LAYER SALAD

SUMMERY GREEN COLESLAW

COURGETTE AND CHICKPEA SALAD

GREEN PASTA

SMOKED TROUT SALAD

QUINOA, PRAWN AND MANGO SALAD

BANG-BANG CHICKEN SALAD

LENTIL AND MERGUEZ SAUSAGE SALAD

LUNCH BOX POT NOODLES

BREAD TARTLETS

CINEMA SNACKS

HARISSA VEGETABLES AND JUMBO COUSCOUS

Jumbo couscous was new to us but it's a wonderful thing – it gives a salad good body and texture. We like this salad by itself for lunch or with some grilled chicken for supper. If you like, you can make this even lower in calories by replacing the couscous with blitzed cauliflower.

Heat the oil in a large frying pan. Add the onions and red peppers and fry them over a high heat for 5 minutes. Add the courgettes, then continue to cook for another couple of minutes.

Add the lemon zest and cumin seeds. Whisk the tomato purée with the harissa paste and the 100ml of stock or water, then pour this over the vegetables and cover the pan. Turn the heat down and simmer for another 5 minutes until the vegetables are softened but still with a bit of bite to them.

While the vegetables are cooking, pour the 500ml of stock or water into a pan, add the couscous and season it with salt and pepper. Bring it to the boil, cover the pan and simmer for 6–8 minutes until the couscous has plumped up and is tender. Remove the pan from the heat and drain off any remaining liquid.

Add the tomatoes to the frying pan with the vegetables and leave them to soften, covered, for a further minute.

Mix the couscous with the salad leaves, then add the vegetables and their dressing. Squeeze over a little lemon juice and sprinkle liberally with the mint and parsley leaves.

SERVES 4

1 tsp olive oil

2 red onions, finely sliced into wedges

2 red peppers, deseeded and cut into strips

2 large courgettes, cut thinly on the diagonal

zest of 1 lemon

1 tsp cumin seeds

1 tbsp tomato purée

1 tbsp harissa paste

100ml hot vegetable stock or water

12 cherry tomatoes, halved

Couscous and salad

500ml vegetable stock

100g jumbo couscous

200g salad leaves

squeeze of lemon juice

handful of mint leaves

handful of parsley leaves

flaked sea salt

freshly ground black pepper

197 calories per serving

SEVEN-LAYER SALAD

This is a pick-and-mix of joy and a feast for your eyes and for your ever-reducing belly. Looks like loads of ingredients we know but there's nothing complicated – just chopping, mixing and assembling. The trad way of serving this is in layers in a big glass bowl but we like to arrange the layers in stripes on a platter.

If using frozen sweetcorn, cook it in boiling water for a couple of minutes, then drain and cool. Shred the lettuce heart, drain and rinse the black beans, and coarsely grate the Cheddar.

To make the tomato salsa, mix the tomatoes, red peppers, red onion and coriander stems in a bowl and sprinkle over the cumin. Season with salt and pepper and add the lime juice. Stir thoroughly.

To make the chicken salad, put the chicken and celery in a bowl. Mix the buttermilk with the mayonnaise and whisk in the white wine vinegar and lime juice. Season with salt and pepper, then stir the buttermilk mixture into the chicken and celery.

For the avocado salad, peel and stone the avocado, then cut the flesh into thin slices. Grate the courgette and finely chop the spring onions. Put them in a bowl, season with salt and pepper and squeeze over the lime juice. Fold together gently so you don't break up the avocado too much.

If you're serving the salad in a glass bowl, put the lettuce in the base, then add the remaining layers – sweetcorn, black beans, tomato salsa, chicken salad, avocado and grated cheese. Put them in whatever order you like, but the grated cheese should be on the top. To serve, mix with salad servers after everyone has seen and admired the layers.

For serving on a platter, arrange the layers in stripes – again, in whatever order you like. No need to mix – just let everyone help themselves.

SERVES 4

200g sweetcorn, canned or frozen

1 romaine lettuce heart

400g can of black beans

25g Cheddar or other hard cheese

Tomato salsa

3 tomatoes, finely chopped

2 roasted red peppers (from a jar), finely chopped

½ small red onion, finely chopped

2 tbsp coriander stems, finely chopped

1 tsp cumin

juice of 1 lime

sea salt

freshly ground black pepper

Chicken salad

3 cooked chicken breasts, skinned and diced

1 celery stick, finely chopped

2 tbsp buttermilk

2 tbsp low-cal mayonnaise

1 tsp white wine or cider vinegar

squeeze of lime juice

Avocado salad

1 avocado

1 courgette

2 spring onions

juice of 1 lime

446 calories per serving

SUMMERY GREEN COLESLAW

Fresh, crunchy and full of flavour, this green coleslaw really smacks of summer. Nice with lots of herbs but add them just before serving, as they start to go black and limp after being torn and chopped. Good with a turkey burger.

SERVES 4

100g frozen peas or baby broad beans, cooked and cooled

1 small green cabbage, shredded

1 large courgette, grated or sliced into matchsticks

1 large fennel bulb, trimmed and sliced into matchsticks

1 bunch of spring onions, finely sliced

2 celery sticks, finely chopped

1 green apple, grated

juice of ½ lime

bunch of basil leaves, torn

bunch of mint leaves, chopped

flaked sea salt

freshly ground black pepper

Dressing

2 tbsp low-fat yoghurt

2 tbsp low-fat mayonnaise

zest and juice of 1 lemon

1 tbsp finely chopped tarragon

pinch of sugar

V   *130 calories per serving*

Bring a pan of water to the boil, add the peas or beans and bring the water back to the boil. Cook for 2 minutes, then drain.

Put the cabbage, courgette, fennel, spring onions and celery in a large bowl and add the cooked peas or broad beans. Mix the grated apple with the lime juice, then add it to the vegetables. Season with salt and pepper, then stir well to combine.

Whisk together all the dressing ingredients and season with salt and pepper. Pour the dressing over the vegetables. Garnish with the basil and mint leaves just before serving.

COURGETTE AND CHICKPEA SALAD

The chickpeas make this a good hearty salad. We like adding broad beans, but if you don't have any it'll still taste good. Or you could add a few green peas instead. The dressing is really tangy and tasty so take the time to make it – trust us, it's worth it. We love the cinnamon which adds a lovely warm hit of Middle Eastern flavour – Morocco comes to Morecambe.

SERVES 4

2 courgettes, trimmed

low-cal oil spray

100g frozen broad beans

1 tbsp olive oil

2 garlic cloves, finely chopped

zest and juice of 1 lemon

1 tsp cumin

pinch of cayenne

pinch of cinnamon

100g rocket leaves

400g can of chickpeas, drained and rinsed

small bunch of mint, chopped

small bunch of basil, torn

flaked sea salt

freshly ground black pepper

V ❄ *143 calories per serving*

Preheat your grill until it's really hot. Meanwhile, cut the courgettes into thin diagonal slices. Spray a baking tray with oil, then arrange the slices of courgette on it and season them with salt and pepper. Grill the courgette slices for 3–4 minutes on each side until nicely browned around the edges.

While the courgettes are grilling, bring a kettle of water to the boil, pour some of the water into a saucepan and bring it back to the boil. Add the broad beans, cook them for about 3 minutes, then drain.

Heat the olive oil in a small frying pan, add the chopped garlic and fry it very briefly making sure it doesn't take on any colour. Add the lemon zest and juice and the spices. Season with salt and pepper. Swirl the pan around a little to combine everything, then remove it from the heat and set aside.

Wash the rocket leaves and put them in a salad bowl. Add the chickpeas to the bowl along with the grilled courgettes and broad beans. Pour the garlicky dressing over the salad and toss, then add the chopped mint and basil leaves. Serve immediately.

Biker tip: If you want to freeze this salad, freeze it without the rocket leaves and herbs. Add them after defrosting.

GREEN PASTA

Pasta and pesto is one of our favourite suppers, but the regular version contains lots of oil, cheese and nuts so is quite rich. Try our healthier, lighter recipe, which cuts down the calories but not the flavour and uses a little of the pasta cooking water to thicken the sauce – classic Italian tip. Eat this warm, or cool as a salad. Makes a great lunch box salad too.

Bring a full kettle of water to the boil, then pour the water into a large saucepan. Put a lid on the pan and bring the water back to the boil, then add plenty of salt and the pasta. Cook the pasta for 10–12 minutes, or until cooked through but still with a bit of bite to it, adding the grated courgette at the last minute.

Put the basil, garlic, oil and lemon zest in a food processor with a small ladleful of the cooking liquor – do this towards the end of the cooking time so the water will have more starch in it. Season with salt and pepper. Blitz the sauce until it's fairly smooth but still flecked with green from the basil.

Drain the pasta and courgette, toss it with the sauce and serve with grated Parmesan cheese.

SERVES 4

200g short pasta

1 large courgette, grated

1 large bunch of basil

1 garlic clove, finely chopped

1 tbsp olive oil

grated zest of 1 lemon

25g Parmesan cheese or a vegetarian alternative, grated

flaked sea salt

freshly ground black pepper

239 calories per serving

SMOKED TROUT SALAD

Fillets of smoked trout make a quick, easy and nourishing salad and the celeriac fries add a crispy crunch. Get those going right away so they can be cooking while your prepare the rest of the salad and you'll be sitting down to a tasty feast in no time. You need hot-smoked trout (or salmon) for this, as it flakes nicely. Thinly sliced fish doesn't work.

SERVES 4

200g celeriac, peeled weight

low-cal oil spray

100g green beans

100g salad leaves, such as spinach, baby kale, pea shoots or lamb's lettuce

250g cooked beetroot, cut into wedges

200g smoked trout

small bunch of dill, leaves only

a few chives

flaked sea salt

freshly ground black pepper

Dressing

75ml buttermilk or low-fat yoghurt

1 tsp cider vinegar

2 tsp Dijon mustard

½ tsp runny honey

135 calories per serving

Preheat the oven to 220°C/Fan 200°C/Gas 7. Cut the celeriac into very fine matchsticks. The easiest way to do this is to cut it into thin slices first, using a mandolin if you have one, and then into fine strips. Spritz a baking tray with low-cal oil and spread the celeriac strips over it. Sprinkle them quite generously with salt, and pepper, then spray with oil again.

Bake the celeriac fries in the oven for 20 minutes, turning them over every 5 minutes or so, until they have shrunk down and cooked through. You will find some strips are well browned and crunchy while others are slightly softer, but the contrast is good. The fries will crisp up further as they cool.

While the celeriac is cooking, prepare the rest of the salad. Trim the green beans and cut them in half. Cook them in a saucepan of boiling water for 4–5 minutes or until tender, then drain.

Spread the salad leaves over a large platter and add the beans, beetroot and celeriac fries.

Break up the trout into chunks and add these to the salad. Separate the dill into small fronds and snip the chives with scissors, then sprinkle them over the salad.

Whisk the salad dressing ingredients together and season with salt and pepper. Drizzle the dressing over the salad and serve.

QUINOA, PRAWN AND MANGO SALAD

Bold, zesty flavours make this a real treat and you wouldn't believe how well the mango and prawns go together. Do your best to allow time to marinate the prawns briefly, as it really does make a difference. The time it takes for the griddle to heat up is long enough. If you fancy, you could add some thinly sliced courgettes or some briefly cooked green beans to this.

SERVES 4

100g quinoa

200ml hot vegetable or chicken stock or water

1 tsp olive oil

grated zest of 1 lime

2 garlic cloves, crushed

400g raw king prawns, shelled

1 mango

1 red chilli, deseeded and roughly chopped

5g fresh root ginger, roughly chopped

1 tsp white wine vinegar

juice of 1 lime

200g salad leaves, such as rocket, baby spinach or lamb's lettuce

4 spring onions, cut into 2cm diagonal slices

small bunch of coriander, leaves only

a few basil leaves

flaked sea salt

freshly ground black pepper

200 calories per serving

Rinse the quinoa thoroughly under running water, then drain it well. Put the quinoa in a saucepan and cook it over a medium heat for a minute to help develop a nutty flavour, then pour over the stock or water. Season with salt and pepper. Bring the liquid to the boil, then cover the pan and turn the heat down to a simmer. Cook for 15 minutes, then remove the pan from the heat and leave the quinoa to stand for 5 minutes. Remove the lid and leave to cool for a few minutes.

Meanwhile, get on with the rest of the salad. Place a griddle on the hob to heat up. Put the olive oil in a bowl with the lime zest and add the crushed garlic. Add the prawns and season them with salt and pepper, then leave them to marinate and absorb the flavours for 5 minutes. By then, the griddle should be good and hot so cook the prawns for a minute or so on each side until they are pink. Set them aside.

Peel the mango. Cut half the flesh into strips or cubes for the salad and set them aside. Put the rest of the flesh into a blender or food processor, squeezing the big seed between your hands to get any further juice. Add the chilli and ginger to the blender, together with the white wine vinegar and lime juice, then season with salt and pepper. Blitz until smooth to make the dressing.

To serve, arrange the salad leaves on a large platter and sprinkle the quinoa on top. Add the spring onions and half the herbs, then top with the reserved mango and griddled prawns. Drizzle over the mango and chilli dressing, sprinkle with the rest of the herbs and serve immediately.

BANG-BANG CHICKEN SALAD

This really is banging – a good substantial chicken salad that everyone is going to love.
And you'll have most of the stuff for the sauce in your cupboard. To make this even quicker,
use leftover chicken or bought chicken breasts and just shred them into the peanut sauce.
Super tasty and more bangs for your buck.

Cut the chicken into thin slices and put them in a bowl. Sprinkle over the Chinese five-spice powder and rub it into the chicken.

Add the oil to a wok and place it over the heat. When the oil in the wok is shimmering, add the chicken and fry it briskly for 2–3 minutes until it is cooked through. Pour over the soy sauce and cook for a further minute. Remove the chicken from the wok and put it on a plate to cool down a little.

Now make the peanut sauce. Heat the vegetable oil in the wok and add the shallot or onion, garlic and ginger. Stir-fry for a couple of minutes over a very high heat, then add all the remaining sauce ingredients. Simmer until the sauce is slightly syrupy and well combined, then leave to cool while you make the salad.

Arrange the cabbage, carrot, courgette, bean sprouts and spring onions on a large platter. Add the chicken, then drizzle over the peanut sauce. Sprinkle with the chillies and some coriander leaves.

SERVES 4

400g skinless chicken breasts

1 tsp Chinese five-spice powder

1 tsp vegetable oil

1 tbsp soy sauce

Peanut sauce

1 tsp vegetable oil

1 shallot or small onion, finely chopped

2 garlic cloves, finely chopped

10g fresh root ginger, grated

1 tsp hot sauce

200ml hot chicken stock

1 tbsp lime juice

1 tbsp soy sauce

1 tsp runny honey

1 tbsp crunchy peanut butter

a few drops of sesame oil

Salad

1 large Chinese cabbage, shredded

1 carrot, cut into matchsticks

1 courgette, cut into matchsticks

50g bean sprouts

bunch of spring onions, shredded

2 red chillies, deseeded and finely sliced

small bunch of coriander, leaves only

208 calories per serving

LENTIL AND MERGUEZ SAUSAGE SALAD

Lentils and sausages always work well together and this salad is no exception – it's particularly good served warm. The dressing is fab and there's no oil so it's nice and low cal.

SERVES 4

1 small red onion, sliced into crescents

pinch of sea salt

6 merguez sausages, sliced fairly thinly on the diagonal

200g baby spinach, well washed

250g cooked green or puy lentils (from a can or pack)

1 red pepper, deseeded and diced

2 tbsp finely chopped parsley

Dressing

200g cherry tomatoes, cut into quarters

1 tsp mustard

2 tsp red wine vinegar

pinch of sugar

flaked sea salt

freshly ground black pepper

319 calories per serving

Heat a griddle pan for at least 5 minutes until it's extremely hot. Put the onion in a small bowl, sprinkle it with salt and pour over some cold water. Leave it to stand for 5 minutes, then drain.

Grill the sausages on the hot griddle for a couple of minutes on each side, until cooked through and well charred. Remove them from the heat and set aside.

Divide the spinach between 4 plates. Arrange the lentils, red pepper and drained red onion over the spinach, then top with the cooked sliced sausages.

For the dressing, put the tomatoes in a frying pan and warm them through until they start giving out juice. Whisk the mustard, red wine vinegar and sugar into the juices and cook for a further minute or so. Season with salt and pepper.

Drizzle the tomato dressing over the salad and sausages, then sprinkle with parsley and serve immediately.

Biker tip: If you want to freeze this salad, freeze it without the rocket leaves and herbs and add them after defrosting.

LUNCH BOX POT NOODLES

Take this to the office for your lunch and your workmates will look on in envy. We've suggested three different seasonings and you'll probably come up with your own variations too – let us know! It's really important to use the right kind of noodles – you want the sort that will cook in two or three minutes. Vary the veggies as you like but choose things that cook in about the same time as the noodles. No need to defrost the peas, as they will defrost when you add the hot water.

SERVES 2

2 small nests of quick-cook noodles

1 small carrot

1 small courgette

½ red pepper

2 spring onions

4 mushrooms

1 garlic clove, finely chopped

5g fresh root ginger, finely chopped

2 tbsp frozen peas

50g cooked chicken

small bunch of fresh coriander

flaked sea salt

freshly ground black pepper

Thai seasoning

1 chicken stock cube, crumbled

1 tbsp Thai green curry paste

1 tbsp fish sauce

juice of 1 lime

Miso seasoning

1 tbsp instant miso

a few thin strips of nori seaweed

1 tbsp tamari or soy sauce

Chinese seasoning

1 tsp Chinese five-spice powder

1 chicken stock cube, crumbled

1 tbsp soy sauce

Divide the noodles between 2 large, lidded, heatproof jars.

Grate the carrot and cut the courgette and red pepper into thin matchsticks. Thinly slice the spring onions and the mushrooms. Layer the vegetables on top of the noodles, then sprinkle over the garlic and ginger, followed by the peas. Finely dice or shred the chicken and add this too, then top with some coriander leaves.

Add the ingredients for your choice of seasoning – Thai, miso or Chinese – and a little salt and black pepper. Seal with the lid. When you are ready to cook your pot noodles, pour over freshly boiled hot water. Leave the lid sitting on top and leave for 4–5 minutes, prodding regularly with a fork or a chopstick so the seasonings mix and dissolve into the water.

When the noodles have softened, continue to mix, then eat while still hot. Season with some extra soy, fish sauce and lime juice if you like.

322 calories per serving

BREAD TARTLETS

These mini-quiches for dieters make a cracking savoury snack – and we've come up with a cheeky sweet version too! Once you cut rounds out of the slices of bread you will have quite a lot of trimmings. We don't like waste so we leave them to dry out, blitz them to breadcrumbs and stash them in the freezer to use another time.

MAKES 8

low-cal oil spray

8 slices of white sandwich bread or thick sliced bread

75g half-fat crème fraiche

1 egg

1–2 tsp Dijon mustard

40g cooked ham, diced

1 tbsp finely chopped parsley

20g Cheddar cheese, grated (optional)

flaked sea salt

freshly ground black pepper

134 calories per tartlet

Preheat the oven to 220°C/Fan 200°C/Gas 7. Spray a fairy cake tin with oil. Cut the crusts off the slices of bread and roll each slice flat with a rolling pin. Cut out rounds using a 7.5–8cm pastry cutter.

Press the rounds into the fairy cake moulds – when firmly in the corners the sides should still reach the top of the tin. Spray the bread cases with oil again, then bake them for 7–8 minutes until crisp but with very little colour.

Meanwhile, whisk the crème fraiche and egg together until smooth and season with salt and pepper.

When the tartlet cases have finished baking, remove them from the oven, leaving the oven on. Dollop a small amount of mustard in the centre of each tartlet and spread it over the base. Add a little ham, then spoon in some of the crème fraiche and egg mixture, filling the tarts right to the top. Sprinkle with parsley and grated cheese, if using. Put the tartlets back in the oven and bake for about 10 minutes until just set.

Biker tip: We couldn't resist trying a sweet version of these. Make the cases as above. While they're baking, mix 60g of half-fat crème fraiche with 1 egg and a tablespoon of maple syrup. Fill the tartlets and top with a grating of nutmeg, then bake as above – 133 calories each.

CINEMA SNACKS

SERVES 6

BAKED TORTILLA CHIPS

4 corn tortillas

sea salt

25g Cheddar cheese or a vegetarian
alternative, grated (optional)

Spice mix (optional)

1 tsp cumin

1 tsp chilli powder

1 tsp garlic or onion granules

zest of 1 lime

1 tsp salt

Salsa

3 medium red tomatoes

1 small red onion

2 tbsp chopped coriander leaves

juice of 1 lime

½ tsp cumin

1 tsp chipotle paste or hot sauce

V *170 calories per serving (with salsa)*

Preheat the oven to 200°C/Fan 180°C/Gas 6. Cut each of the
tortillas into 3 pieces horizontally so you have 2 half moons and
1 rectangle. Cut each half moon into 3 triangles, then the rectangle
into 6 triangles.

Arrange the pieces on a couple of baking trays and sprinkle them
with salt. If you are using the cheese, sprinkle it over the tortilla
chips. For the spice mix, combine the spices and garlic with the
lime zest and a teaspoon of salt and sprinkle this over the chips.

Bake the chips for 8–10 minutes until golden brown in places and
crisp and dry. They will continue to crisp up as they cool down.

While the chips are in the oven, make the salsa. Finely chop the
tomatoes and onion and put them in a bowl with the coriander and
lime juice. Stir in the cumin and chipotle paste or hot sauce and
season with salt if needed. Serve with the chips.

SERVES 4

SPICED POPCORN

1 tsp vegetable oil

75g popping corn

1 tsp mild chilli powder

zest of 1 lime

1 tsp salt

1 tbsp lime juice

V *81 calories per serving*

Heat the oil in a large lidded saucepan. Add the popping corn
and put the lid on the pan. Cook over a medium heat for about
4–5 minutes, shaking regularly when the corn starts popping,
and holding down the lid.

When the popping has stopped completely (when you go for
about 15 seconds without hearing any sound), it will be safe to
remove the lid. Tip the popcorn into a bowl, discarding any
kernels that haven't popped.

Mix the chilli powder, lime zest and salt together. Shake this
mixture over the popcorn, making sure it is all well dusted,
then sprinkle over the lime juice.

FULLER FASTER

SPICY SWEETCORN FRITTERS

HAM AND PEA FRITTERS

GRILLED AUBERGINES WITH CHICKPEA AND SPINACH SALAD

WHITE BEAN AND TUNA FISHCAKES

MARINATED FISH WITH STIR-FRIED GREENS

BAKED FISH WITH GREEN AND WHITE BEANS

FISH VÉRONIQUE

CHILLI PRAWN PASTA

GRILLED CHICKEN WITH FENNEL SAUCE

SZECHUAN CHICKEN STIR-FRY

CHICKEN LIVERS – ESCABECHE STYLE

PORK MEDALLIONS IN BBQ SAUCE

LAMB STEAKS WITH MINT AND BROAD BEANS

STEAK WITH CHEAT'S 'BÉARNAISE'

SPICY SWEETCORN FRITTERS

You're going to love our Hairy Biker fitter fritters! These little numbers are good served with salad or slices of ham and also make a nice starter with this tangy dipping sauce.

MAKES 12

300g frozen sweetcorn

3 eggs

1 tbsp soy sauce

1 tsp sriracha hot sauce or similar

60g plain flour

1 tbsp finely chopped coriander stems

1 garlic clove, finely chopped

1 spring onion, finely chopped

low-cal oil spray

flaked sea salt

freshly ground black pepper

Dipping sauce

2 tbsp soy sauce

juice of 1 lime

½ tsp sugar or honey

1 tsp red chilli flakes

1 garlic clove, finely chopped

57 calories per fritter

Bring a kettle of water to the boil. Put the sweetcorn in a heatproof bowl, pour over some boiling water and leave for a minute or so while the sweetcorn defrosts. Drain and set aside.

Crack the eggs into a separate bowl and beat them until well broken up. Add the soy sauce and hot sauce and season with salt and pepper. Sprinkle over the plain flour and whisk to combine, making sure there are no lumps. Add the coriander stems, garlic, spring onion and sweetcorn to the batter and stir thoroughly.

Heat a large frying pan and spray with oil, covering the base as evenly as possible. Dollop heaped tablespoons of the batter on to the pan, spacing them out well. You should be able to cook 4 or 5 fritters at once, but don't be tempted to crowd the pan or it will be hard to turn them. Cook the fritters for 2–3 minutes until well browned underneath, then flip them and cook on the other side. Remove the fritters from the pan and set them aside to keep warm while you cook the rest.

While the fritters are cooking, make the dipping sauce. Put the soy sauce and lime juice in a small bowl, add the sugar or honey and stir until completely dissolved. Add the chilli flakes and garlic, then leave to stand until ready to serve.

HAM AND PEA FRITTERS

It's the peas that give these fritters their amazing colour and they are superb, we promise you. Like the sweetcorn fritters, these are good on their own with a little sauce or served up with some veg, salad or whatever you fancy.

MAKES 12

300g frozen peas
60g plain flour
1 tsp baking powder
2 eggs
2 tbsp milk
100g cooked ham, diced
low-cal oil spray
flaked sea salt
freshly ground black pepper

Mustard sauce
1 tsp ready-made mustard
4 tbsp 0% fat natural yoghurt

69 calories per fritter

Put the peas in a sieve and run hot water over them to defrost. Bring a kettle of water to the boil, then pour some into a small saucepan. Add the peas, bring the water back to the boil and cook for 2 minutes. Drain the peas, then purée them roughly – you want a mixture of whole and crushed peas. You can do this in a food processor or simply mash the peas in a bowl.

Put the plain flour in a large bowl with the baking powder and season with salt and pepper. Make a well in the flour and break in the eggs. Break up the eggs with a fork and start working in the flour from the sides of the bowl until it is all mixed in. Add the milk and whisk to make a smooth batter. Stir in the peas and ham.

Heat a large, shallow non-stick frying pan and spray the base with oil. Add tablespoons of the batter, spacing them out well. You should be able to cook 4 or 5 at a time but don't overcrowd the pan. Cook the fritters for 2–3 minutes until they are well browned underneath, then flip them and cook them on the other side. Remove the fritters from the pan and set them aside to keep warm while you cook the rest.

Stir the mustard into the yoghurt to make the sauce and serve with the fritters.

GRILLED AUBERGINES WITH CHICKPEA AND SPINACH SALAD

The aubergines make a great starter just with the yoghurt sauce but they're even better with the chickpea salad too. This is a good vegetarian dish, but check the feta you're using is suitable and not made with animal rennet.

Put the grill on to heat up to its highest setting while you prepare the aubergines. Top and tail the aubergines, making sure you cut at least 1cm away from the top, as this can be a bit tough. Cut the aubergines into ½cm slices. You should get at least 12 good-sized slices from each aubergine, as well as the smaller end bits.

Spritz 2 non-stick baking trays with low-cal oil spray and arrange the aubergine slices on the trays. Spray the aubergines with oil and season them with salt and pepper. Place one of the trays under the grill, preferably on the second shelf down (they will burn if right at the top), then grill the slices for 5 minutes. Turn them over and grill for another 5 minutes or 3 minutes if adding feta.

If using feta, crumble half of it over the grilled aubergine slices, then grill for a further 2 minutes. Remove the tray from the grill, then cook the second batch in the same way.

While the aubergines are grilling, make the yoghurt dressing. Soak the saffron in the hot water for 5 minutes. Whisk the saffron and its soaking liquor into the yoghurt with the garlic and dried mint. Season with salt and pepper and serve with the aubergine slices and the chickpea and spinach salad.

Chickpea and spinach salad

Heat the oil in a large saucepan and add the garlic. Cook it for a minute, then add the chickpeas, cumin, lemon zest and 50ml of water. Season with salt and pepper and leave to simmer over a low heat until warmed through.

Thoroughly wash the spinach and shake it briefly to get rid of any excess water. Add the spinach to the pan, pushing it down as it wilts. Leave it for a couple of minutes to combine with the chickpeas, then stir.

SERVES 4

3 medium aubergines

low-cal oil spray

50g feta cheese (optional)

flaked sea salt

freshly ground black pepper

Yoghurt dressing

large pinch of saffron

30ml hot water

200g low-fat or 0% fat Greek yoghurt

1 garlic clove, crushed

1 tsp dried mint

Chickpea and spinach salad

1 tsp olive oil

1 garlic clove, finely chopped

400g can of chickpeas, drained and rinsed

1 tsp ground cumin

grated zest of 1 lemon

200g fresh baby leaf spinach

205 calories per serving V

WHITE BEAN AND TUNA FISHCAKES

Everyone loves a fishcake, and tuna and white beans are a classic combo. You can use any kind of canned fish for these – salmon, sardines, mackerel – as long as it's packed in spring water, as this reduces the calories by a lot. BTW, you might be tempted to throw everything into the food processor at once, but don't. We've tried doing this different ways and it really is worth blitzing the beans and the fish separately to get the right texture – otherwise the beans get too smooth and claggy. And you don't need to wash the food processor in between so it doesn't take much longer.

Preheat the oven to 220°C/Fan 200°C/Gas 7. Put the beans in a food processor and pulse a few times until they have broken down a little but are not completely puréed. You want a fairly coarse but uniform texture. Tip the beans into a large bowl.

Put the fish in the food processor with the onion and parsley and blitz until everything is well combined and the parsley is very finely chopped. Add this mixture to the bowl with the beans.

Add the mustard, egg, lemon zest and juice to the beans and fish, and season generously with salt and pepper. Mix thoroughly, then taste again for seasoning.

Sprinkle the panko breadcrumbs over a plate. Shape the fish and bean mixture into 8 patties, dip them in the breadcrumbs, then pat off any excess. Spritz a non-stick baking tray with low-cal oil spray and place the fishcakes on it. Spray the top of the fishcakes with oil.

Bake the fishcakes in the oven for about 15 minutes, turning them halfway through the cooking time.

While the fishcakes are baking, make the sauce. Simply mix all the ingredients in a bowl and stir well, then season with salt and black pepper.

MAKES 8 FISHCAKES

2 x 400g cans of cannellini beans, drained and rinsed

2 cans of fish in spring water, drained weight 200–250g

1 onion, very finely chopped

small bunch of parsley, roughly chopped

2 tsp Dijon mustard

1 egg, beaten

grated zest and juice of 1 lemon

100g panko breadcrumbs

low-cal oil spray

flaked sea salt

freshly ground black pepper

Sauce (optional)

grated zest and juice of 1 lemon

1 tbsp finely chopped capers

1 tbsp finely chopped cornichons

1 tbsp Dijon mustard

150ml 0%-fat yoghurt

175 calories per fishcake

MARINATED FISH WITH STIR-FRIED GREENS

We love our fish and this excellent dish has become a firm favourite of ours. We did want to make it a one-pot but instead it's a two-pot wonder. Just works better if the fish and veggies are cooked separately. And don't forget – that extra bit of washing-up burns calories.

SERVES 4

juice of 1 orange

3 tbsp soy sauce

1 tsp runny honey

10g fresh root ginger

2 garlic cloves

4 x 150g skinless salmon fillets

2 tsp vegetable oil

low-cal oil spray

1 tsp sesame oil

2 tsp sesame seeds

flaked sea salt

freshly ground black pepper

Stir-fried greens

2 tsp vegetable oil

6 spring onions, cut into rounds

1 green pepper, finely diced

1 red chilli, finely diced

1 green pointed cabbage or similar, cut into quarters and shredded

441 calories per serving

Put the orange juice in a bowl with the soy sauce and honey. Grate the ginger and crush the garlic into the bowl. Whisk thoroughly to combine and dissolve the honey, then season with salt and pepper.

Put the salmon in the bowl and coat it with the marinade. Leave to stand for a few minutes.

Heat the vegetable oil in a wok. When the oil in the wok starts to shimmer, add all the stir-fry ingredients and cook them for 2–3 minutes. Turn down the heat slightly.

While the vegetables are cooking, remove the salmon fillets from the bowl and put them on some kitchen paper to drain. Reserve the marinade. Spray a frying pan with low-cal oil and place it over a medium heat. Put the salmon fillets in the frying pan and cook them for 2–3 minutes on one side, then turn them over.

Add a tablespoon of the marinade to the vegetables in the wok and allow them to simmer for a few minutes. Pour the remaining marinade around the salmon – it should reduce to a thin syrup while the salmon is cooking. Flip the salmon over one more time just to get a coating of the reduced marinade.

Drizzle the sesame oil over the vegetables and divide them between 4 plates. Add the salmon and drizzle over any remaining marinade. Sprinkle with sesame seeds and serve immediately.

BAKED FISH WITH GREEN AND WHITE BEANS

This is a lovely comforting supper dish and it's very easy to put together. It works best with a nice thick piece of white fish.

SERVES 4

4 x 150g white fish fillets (cod or haddock)

200g green beans, trimmed and halved

1 tbsp olive oil

1 small red onion, finely sliced into crescents

2 garlic cloves, finely chopped

grated zest of 1 lemon

100g cherry tomatoes, halved

2 x 400g cans of cannellini beans, drained and rinsed

bunch of basil, leaves torn

flaked sea salt

freshly ground black pepper

---

315 calories per serving

Preheat the oven to 200°C/Fan 180°C/Gas 6. Line a baking tray with baking parchment, put the fish fillets on the tray and season them with salt and pepper.

Bring a kettle of water to the boil. Pour the water into a saucepan and bring it back to the boil. Add the green beans and cook them for 3–4 minutes until they're just done. Drain the beans and set them aside.

While the beans are cooking, start on the sauce. Heat the olive oil in a large saucepan while you prepare the onion and garlic. Add the onion to the pan and cook it gently over a medium heat for a few minutes – you want it to colour a little but still have some bite. Then add the garlic and lemon zest and cook for another minute.

Put the fish in the oven and bake it for 12–15 minutes.

While the fish is cooking, finish the sauce. Add the tomatoes to the saucepan with the onion and garlic, along with the cannellini beans and the green beans. Season with salt and pepper. Cook gently for a few minutes until the tomatoes have just warmed through and have started to release some of their juices.

When the fish is cooked serve it with the beans, liberally sprinkled with torn basil leaves.

Biker tip: If you do have a bit longer than half an hour, you could brine the fish before baking. It only takes 20 minutes and it firms the fish up nicely. Mix one part of salt with 9 parts of water in a bowl. Add the fish and leave for 20 minutes, then drain well.

FISH VÉRONIQUE

We're very happy that we can enjoy this dieter's version of a French classic and we think you will be too. It's traditionally made with Dover sole, but that's expensive so we use lemon sole instead. Other options are tilapia, plaice or any other white fish that keeps its shape and doesn't flake away to nothing. Ask the people at your fish counter to skin the fillets for you.

SERVES 4

5g butter

1 shallot, very finely chopped

100ml vermouth or white wine

250ml hot fish stock

2 large sprigs of tarragon, plus 2 tbsp finely chopped tarragon leaves

200g white grapes

100ml single cream

600g thin white fish fillets, skinned

flaked sea salt

white pepper

231 calories per serving

Melt the butter in a large frying pan that has a lid. Add the shallot and cook it over a low heat for 5 minutes until it's starting to soften. Pour the vermouth or white wine into the pan and let it boil for a minute, then add the fish stock along with the sprigs of tarragon. Bring the liquid back to the boil and cook it quite vigorously for 5 minutes until it's reduced by about a third.

Cut the grapes in half, add them to the pan and simmer them for a couple of minutes, then pour in the single cream. Season with salt and white pepper, add the finely chopped tarragon leaves and stir to combine. Continue to simmer the sauce for a couple of minutes until it has a consistency slightly thicker than single cream.

Cut the fish fillets in half lengthways, then slice each diagonally across the middle.

Carefully arrange the pieces of fish over the sauce. Put the lid on the pan and simmer for another 3–4 minutes, until the fish has just cooked. Serve immediately.

CHILLI PRAWN PASTA

With chilli, garlic and lime, this pasta dish is brimming with bold flavours and makes a proper filling dinner. If you do happen to have some vodka handy, we recommend adding a dash. It works a bit of extra magic.

SERVES 4

200g spaghetti

1 small onion, finely chopped

1 red pepper, deseeded and finely chopped

2 garlic cloves, finely chopped

1 tbsp olive oil

1 tsp chilli flakes

grated zest of 1 lime

100ml hot fish or vegetable stock

250ml tomato passata

50ml vodka (optional)

400g shelled raw prawns (defrosted if frozen)

small bunch of coriander or basil

lime wedges, for serving

flaked sea salt

freshly ground black pepper

341 calories per serving

Start by putting a full kettle of water on to boil. Pour the boiled water into a large saucepan, put a lid on the pan and bring the water back to the boil. Season with plenty of salt, then add the spaghetti. Cook for 10–12 minutes until the pasta is tender but still has a little bite to it, then drain.

Meanwhile, prepare the onion, pepper and garlic. Heat the olive oil in a large lidded frying pan, then add the onion and red pepper along with a splash of water. Cover the pan and cook over a medium heat until the veg are starting to soften. Add the garlic, chilli flakes and lime zest, then season with salt and pepper. Pour the stock into the pan, put the lid back on and cook the sauce for another 5 minutes.

Pour in the passata and simmer for a further 5 minutes. Add the vodka, if using, then simmer for a minute or so more. Throw in the prawns and cook until they have just turned pink and opaque – they should still be quite bouncy.

Serve the sauce with the pasta and a sprinkling of coriander or basil leaves to garnish. Add some lime wedges for everyone to squeeze over their helping.

GRILLED CHICKEN WITH FENNEL SAUCE

We use butterflied chicken breasts here – that means breasts that are cut halfway through the middle and opened out so they are nice and thin and cook quickly. This isn't hard to do, but if you ask at your butcher's shop or meat counter they might prepare them for you. If you don't have a large enough griddle to cook all the chicken breasts at once, do them in batches, starting before you cook the fennel.

First prepare the chicken. Place a breast on the work surface, with the top side (the side that would have had the skin attached to it) facing up. Put one hand on top of the chicken breast and take a sharp knife in your other hand. Slice into one side of the breast and keep on slicing through horizontally until you are nearly, but not quite, through to the other side. Now open up the chicken and press the centre flat – it will look like a cross between a butterfly and a love heart. Repeat with the remaining breasts.

Put the chicken breasts in a bowl and season them well with salt. Whisk the oil and lemon juice together and pour them over the chicken. Using your hands, rub the mixture into the chicken, then set the bowl aside. Wash your hands thoroughly.

For the sauce, trim the fennel, reserving any fronds for a garnish, and dice it quite finely. Melt the butter in a small pan and add the fennel. Cook it over a high heat for a couple of minutes, then turn the heat down, cover the pan and leave the fennel to braise gently for 8–10 minutes until it's translucent and almost tender.

While the fennel is braising, finely dice the tomatoes. Put a griddle pan to heat up for several minutes.

Turn up the heat under the pan of fennel and add the vermouth or white wine. Boil until it's reduced down by half, then add the lemon zest and tomatoes. Season with salt and pepper, then leave to simmer for 5 minutes. Tear the basil leaves and stir them into the sauce, then remove the pan from the heat.

Arrange the opened-out chicken breasts on a griddle. Cook them for 3–4 minutes on each side until they have charred lines across their surface and are cooked through. Serve the chicken with the sauce, garnished with a few fennel fronds saved from the bulb.

SERVES 4

4 skinless chicken breasts

1 tsp olive oil

juice of ½ lemon

flaked sea salt

freshly ground black pepper

Fennel sauce

1 large fennel bulb

10g butter

2 large tomatoes, finely diced

50ml vermouth or white wine

grated zest of 1 lemon

a few basil leaves

220 calories per serving

SZECHUAN CHICKEN STIR-FRY

At only 200 calories per serving, you can afford to have a bit of rice alongside this spicy stir-fry. But not too much – rice is what makes Sumo wrestlers fat.

First prepare the chicken. Slice the meat into thin strips, trimming off any visible fat. Cut the woody ends off the asparagus, then slice the stems into lengths of about 5cm. Finely chop the garlic cloves and ginger, then cut the spring onions into thin rounds. Lightly crush the Szechuan and black peppercorns together.

Whisk together all the sauce ingredients until the honey has dissolved.

Heat the vegetable oil in a wok until smoking. Add the strips of chicken and cook them for 3 minutes, stirring constantly, then add the asparagus and baby corn. Continue to cook for a further 2 minutes, then add the garlic, ginger and spring onions. After another minute, add the crushed peppercorns and cayenne or chilli, if using.

Pour the sauce over the chicken and cook for a few minutes more until everything is cooked through and the sauce has reduced a little. Garnish with a few coriander leaves and sesame seeds, if using. Serve with noodles or rice if you like, but don't forget to add the extra calories to your total.

SERVES 4

500g skinless chicken breast or thigh fillets

200g asparagus spears

2 garlic cloves

5g fresh root ginger

4 spring onions

1 tsp Szechuan peppercorns

1 tsp black peppercorns

2 tsp vegetable oil

200g baby corn

½ tsp cayenne or red chilli pepper (optional)

Sauce

2 tbsp soy sauce

1 tbsp rice wine vinegar

1 tsp runny honey

100ml chicken stock

1 tsp sesame oil

Garnish

coriander leaves

1 tsp white or black sesame seeds (optional)

200 calories per serving

CHICKEN LIVERS – ESCABECHE STYLE

Chicken livers are cheap, nourishing and cook really fast. What's more they're full of flavour and we think they should be used more than they are. Escabeche is kind of like a warm pickle and is popular in Latin America. This dish encapsulates those sweet, savoury and sour escabeche flavours that we love in a healthy way. Trust us – it's good.

Heat a teaspoon of the olive oil in a large lidded frying pan and add the onions and red peppers. Cook them over a high heat for a couple of minutes, then add a splash of water, cover the pan and turn down the heat. Leave to cook for 5 minutes.

Add the garlic and cook for a further minute, then remove the onions, peppers and garlic from the pan and set them aside. Add the remaining olive oil to the pan and turn the heat up high. Add the chicken livers and cook them for 2 minutes on each side, then put the onions, peppers and garlic back in the pan.

Whisk the sherry vinegar, Tabasco, honey, tomato purée and chicken stock together in a small bowl and pour the mixture over the chicken livers. Leave to simmer for a few minutes to make sure the livers are cooked through and the vegetables have softened nicely. Sprinkle with plenty of oregano or parsley leaves and serve.

SERVES 4

2 tsp olive oil

2 red onions, sliced into thin wedges

2 red peppers, deseeded and sliced

2 garlic cloves, finely chopped

400g chicken livers, trimmed

1 tbsp sherry or red wine vinegar

dash of Tabasco sauce

½ tsp runny honey

1 tbsp tomato purée

100ml chicken stock

fresh oregano or parsley

167 calories per serving

PORK MEDALLIONS IN BBQ SAUCE

Kids love this – we love this – and it makes a dead tasty supper. Some green veg is good alongside the pork and maybe some sweet potato mash – it echoes the sweetness of the pork nicely. Or the sweetcorn fritters (see page 86) would work well too. Be sure to have the pan really good and hot for searing the meat and a word of caution – don't cook the medallions for too long or they could be dry.

SERVES 4

1 pork tenderloin (about 600g), trimmed of fat

2 tsp vegetable oil

flaked sea salt

freshly ground black pepper

BBQ sauce

½ onion, roughly chopped

3 garlic cloves, roughly chopped

1 tbsp red wine vinegar

1 tbsp tomato purée

1 tbsp Worcestershire sauce

1 tbsp dark soy sauce

juice of 1 orange

250ml chicken stock

1 tbsp maple syrup (optional)

½ tsp hot sauce (optional)

239 calories per serving

Cut the tenderloin into 1½–2cm slices – you should get about 16 pieces. Season the meat with salt and pepper, then set it aside for a few minutes.

For the sauce, put the onion and garlic in a blender or food processor with the red wine vinegar, tomato purée, Worcestershire sauce and soy sauce. Season with salt and pepper, then blitz until you have a smooth sauce. Tip this into a small saucepan and add the orange juice, stock, maple syrup and the hot sauce, if using.

Bring the mixture to the boil and allow it to bubble quite fiercely for 10 minutes or until it has reduced by a half to a third and is thick and syrupy. Keep stirring the sauce regularly to make sure it doesn't catch on the bottom of the pan. Turn down the heat and leave the sauce to simmer while you start cooking the pork.

Heat the vegetable oil in a large frying pan. Add the pork slices and sear them on each side for a minute. You'll probably need to do this in batches so you don't overcrowd the pan. When all the slices are seared, put them back into the pan. Pour over the sauce and leave the pork to simmer for at least 5 minutes, until it's cooked through and has added flavour to the sauce.

LAMB STEAKS WITH MINT AND BROAD BEANS

We've suggested marinating the lamb steaks briefly for extra flavour here. Yes, marinating and cooking all in half an hour seems a tall order, but it can be done and is well worth it. The broad beans are a perfect accompaniment. We always have some broad beans in the freezer and this method of stewing them with tomatoes and spices turns them into something special.

SERVES 4

4 lamb steaks, about 150g each

2 tsp olive oil

1 tbsp red wine vinegar

2 tsp dried mint

½ tsp sugar, runny honey or pomegranate molasses

1 tsp cumin (optional)

Broad beans

500g frozen broad beans

2 tsp olive oil

1 onion, finely chopped

2 garlic cloves, finely chopped

grated zest of ½ lemon

1 tsp cumin

pinch of cinnamon

1 tsp dried oregano

200ml hot chicken stock or water

200g canned tomatoes

juice of ½ lemon

1 tsp pomegranate molasses (optional)

small bunch of parsley, finely chopped

flaked sea salt

freshly ground black pepper

406 calories per serving

First marinate the lamb. Trim the lamb of any fat. Whisk the olive oil and red wine vinegar in a bowl with the mint, sugar, honey or pomegranate molasses and the cumin, if using. Rub the mixture into the lamb steaks and leave them for at least 10 minutes, preferably a little longer. (If you have the chance to do this in advance, so much the better.)

While the lamb is marinating, get on with the beans. Put the broad beans in a heatproof bowl, pour some boiling water over them and leave for a minute or so while the beans defrost. Drain and set aside.

Heat the olive oil in a saucepan and add the onion. Cook gently over a medium heat for a few minutes, then add the garlic, lemon zest, spices and oregano. Season with salt and pepper, then add the broad beans and the stock or water. Bring to the boil, then turn down the heat, cover the pan with a lid and cook for 5 minutes.

At this point, put a griddle pan on the hob to heat up – it will need at least 5 minutes.

Add the tomatoes, lemon juice and pomegranate molasses to the broad beans and leave to simmer gently while you cook the lamb.

Shake off any excess marinade from the lamb steaks, then place them on the griddle. Cook for 2–3 minutes on each side until well charred on the outside but still pink in the middle. Remove from the griddle and allow them to rest for a few minutes.

Serve the lamb steaks with the broad beans, garnished with finely chopped parsley.

STEAK WITH CHEAT'S 'BÉARNAISE'

We couldn't do a book on fast food without a steak recipe – the ultimate fast but delicious supper. These steaks are served with our cheat's version of the classic steak sauce – Béarnaise.

SERVES 2

2 thin sirloin steaks, about 150g each, trimmed of fat

Sauce

1 small shallot, finely chopped

small bunch of tarragon, roughly chopped

50ml white wine or vermouth

1 tbsp white wine vinegar

100ml half-fat crème fraiche

2 egg yolks

½ tsp Dijon mustard

a few chives

squeeze of lemon juice

flaked sea salt

white pepper

Tomato and onion salad

2 medium tomatoes, thinly sliced into rounds

½ small red onion, finely chopped

1 tsp olive oil

a few tarragon leaves and chives, finely chopped

First, take your steaks out of the fridge so they can come up to room temperature before you cook them. If you've just got home with them, better still. Just leave them on one side while you start the sauce.

Put the shallot and tarragon in a small saucepan. Add the wine or vermouth and the vinegar, bring to the boil, then boil for a minute. Leave to stand for a few minutes.

Put the griddle pan on the hob so it can start heating up. Season the steaks with salt.

Now make the salad. Prepare the tomatoes and onion and arrange them on a serving plate. Drizzle them with the olive oil, season with salt and pepper and sprinkle with the herbs. Set the salad aside until ready to serve.

To finish the sauce, strain it through a fine sieve and discard the solids, then pour the liquid back into the small saucepan. Add the crème fraiche to the pan and season with salt and white pepper. Heat the sauce until it has loosened, then whisk in the egg yolks and mustard. Add the tarragon mixture, the chives and a squeeze of lemon juice, then whisk very briskly until the sauce becomes frothy. Keep it warm and give it another quick whisk before serving.

Put the steaks on the hot griddle. For medium-rare meat, cook them for 2 minutes on the first side and 1½ minutes on the second; for rare, 1½ minutes on the first side, then 1 minute on the second; for medium, cook the steaks for 2 minutes on each side.

Remove the steaks from the griddle and leave them to rest for 5 minutes before serving with the sauce and the salad.

QUICK FEASTS

THAI VEGETABLE CURRY

BLACK-EYED PEAS AND GREENS

FISH CURRY

FISH CRUMBLE

CHICKEN AND PRAWN LAKSA

TURKEY KEEMA PEAS

STICKY CHICKEN DRUMSTICKS

CAULIFLOWER PILAF

PORK AND BLACK BEAN STEW

BEEF STIR-FRY

AMERICAN BISCUITS

QUICK CORN BREAD

THAI VEGETABLE CURRY

It may seem a stretch to make a curry with a fresh paste in half an hour, but it's perfectly possible and the flavour is fantastic. Obviously you can use shop-bought paste if you prefer. We've included Thai basil which you see in lots of supermarkets now, but don't worry too much if you don't have any – just use a mix of ordinary basil and coriander instead.

SERVES 4

1 tsp coconut or vegetable oil

2 shallots, thinly sliced

400ml reduced-fat coconut milk

200ml hot vegetable stock

2 Kaffir lime leaves, shredded

1 medium aubergine

200g butternut squash

200g green beans

1 large courgette

½ small cauliflower (about 200g

juice of 1 lime

small bunch of coriander leaves

small bunch of Thai basil (optional)

flaked sea salt

freshly ground black pepper

Curry paste

1 red chilli

1 tbsp coriander stems

2 shallots

4 garlic cloves

10g fresh root ginger

2 lemongrass stalks or 1 tbsp lemongrass paste

1 tbsp galangal paste (optional)

1 tbsp soy sauce or tamari

½ tsp turmeric

First prepare the ingredients for the curry paste. Deseed the chilli if you want to decrease the heat. Roughly chop the chilli, coriander stems, shallots and garlic. Peel and chop the ginger. Remove the outer layers of the lemongrass stalks, if using, then roughly chop the soft, white centres.

Put all the paste ingredients into a food processor with some salt and pepper. Add a splash of water and blitz until fairly smooth.

Put the coconut or vegetable oil in a large saucepan. Add the shallots and cook them for a couple of minutes, then add the paste. Stir the paste for 2–3 minutes until it smells very aromatic, then pour in the coconut milk and vegetable stock. Add the lime leaves, season with salt and pepper and leave to simmer gently while you prepare the rest of the ingredients.

Cut the aubergine and butternut squash into fairly large chunks of about 3cm. Add them to the saucepan, cover the pan with a lid and simmer for 5 minutes. Meanwhile, trim the green beans, cut the courgette into chunks and separate the cauliflower into florets, cutting them in half if very large. Add these to the pan, then cover again and simmer for a further 5 minutes.

When all the vegetables are tender, add the lime juice. Taste the curry for seasoning and add more soy sauce or tamari if necessary. Serve sprinkled with coriander leaves and Thai basil leaves, if using.

170 calories per serving

BLACK-EYED PEAS AND GREENS

We love the food of the southern US and this is our version of a Cajun favourite – black-eyed peas and greens. We call 'em black-eyed beans over here but they're the same thing. We use spring greens instead of collard greens and haven't included any pork, although you could add a bit of bacon if you like – and you could use 10 grams of lard instead of the oil if you're not cooking for vegetarians. This is extra good served with corn bread so have a look at our recipe on page 137.

Heat the vegetable oil in a large saucepan or a flameproof casserole dish over a medium heat. Add the onion, celery and green pepper to the pan, turn the heat up high and stir for 5 minutes – the vegetables should be browning nicely by this point.

Sprinkle over the garlic powder and onion powder, if using, and the spices and herbs. Stir for a minute, and then add the beans. Pour over the vegetable stock and season with salt and pepper.

Bring to the boil, cover the pan, then turn down the heat and cook for 5 minutes. During this time, wash and shred the spring greens. Pile these on top of the beans – do not stir at this stage.

Turn the heat up again and cover. After 5 minutes the spring greens will have wilted down a little. Stir to combine with the rest of the ingredients and leave to simmer for a further 5 minutes. Serve with corn bread (see p.137).

Biker tip: If you'd like to freeze this dish, cook it up to the stage of adding the greens. After defrosting, reheat, add the greens and finish as above.

SERVES 4

1 tbsp vegetable oil

1 sweet white onion, diced

2 celery sticks, diced

1 green pepper, deseeded and diced

2 tsp garlic powder

1 tsp onion powder (optional)

1 tsp sweet smoked paprika

1 tsp ground cumin

½ tsp cayenne pepper

1 tsp dried oregano or mixed herbs

2 bay leaves

2 x 400g cans of black-eyed beans, drained and rinsed

500ml hot vegetable stock

200g spring greens

flaked sea salt

freshly ground black pepper

207 calories per serving

FISH CURRY

A hot and sour curry, this has a lovely fresh taste and is very simple to make. What's more, it's so low in calories that you can afford to treat yourself to a chapati as well if you fancy. If you're a curry fan you'll probably have some tamarind paste in your larder, but if not it's available in most supermarkets now and it does add a good tangy flavour.

SERVES 4

1 tbsp coconut or vegetable oil

2 onions, thinly sliced

3 garlic cloves, finely chopped

10g fresh root ginger, finely chopped

4 medium tomatoes or 400g canned chopped tomatoes

1 tbsp Kashmiri chilli powder or 2 tsp sweet paprika and 1 tsp cayenne

2 tsp ground cumin

1 tsp ground coriander

½ tsp turmeric

300ml hot fish stock or water

2 tbsp tamarind paste

juice of 1 lime

½ tsp caster sugar (optional)

600g skinned firm white fish fillets (hake or tilapia)

chopped fresh coriander

flaked sea salt

freshly ground black pepper

Heat the oil in a large shallow pan. You need one that has a lid and is wide enough to take all the fish in one layer. Add the onions and stir to coat them with the oil. Cover the pan and leave the onions over a low heat for 5 minutes to start softening while you prepare the garlic and ginger.

If using fresh tomatoes, remove the cores, then blitz them in a blender and set them aside.

Add the garlic and ginger to the onions and cook for a further minute. Sprinkle the spices into the pan and stir briefly to combine. Add the hot fish stock or water and season with salt and pepper. Simmer for 5 minutes, then add the tomatoes and tamarind paste. Bring the curry to the boil, then turn down the heat and leave to cook uncovered for another 5 minutes.

Add the lime juice, then taste the curry and if it seems a little too sour, add the sugar. Cut the fish into large chunks and sit these on top of the sauce, pressing them down very lightly. Cover the pan and cook for 3–4 minutes or until the fish is cooked through. Sprinkle with chopped coriander and serve at once.

226 calories per serving

FISH CRUMBLE

The only thing that's humble about this crumble is the calorie count! Cod, haddock or hake all work well and the smoked fish adds extra flavour. The creamy sauce contrasts brilliantly with the crunchy couscous topping – which we reckon is genius.

SERVES 4

600g skinless white fish fillets, cut into chunks

150g smoked haddock fillets, cut into chunks

low-cal oil spray

flaked sea salt

white pepper

Sauce

1 slice of onion

2 bay leaves

a few white peppercorns

50ml white wine

50ml milk

200ml half-fat crème fraiche

1 tsp plain flour

25g reduced-fat extra-mature Cheddar cheese

small bunch of parsley

Couscous topping

100g couscous

120ml just-boiled water

25g reduced-fat extra-mature Cheddar cheese

2 tsp olive oil

First put the oven on at 200°C/Fan 180°C/Gas 6 to heat up. Tip the couscous into a heatproof bowl and cover with the just-boiled water. Cover and leave the couscous to stand until all the water has been absorbed, then fluff it up with a fork.

For the sauce, put the onion and bay leaves in a saucepan with the peppercorns. Pour in the wine and milk, then stir in the crème fraiche. Put the pan over a low heat and whisk in the flour and cheese. When the sauce is well combined and the cheese has melted, leave to simmer gently for a couple of minutes, then add the fish. Continue to simmer for 3–4 minutes until the fish is just cooked through.

Finely chop the parsley and set aside 2 tablespoons. Stir the rest into the sauce. Spray a shallow ovenproof dish with oil. Spoon the fish and sauce into the dish and season with salt and white pepper.

Now add the topping. Mix the reserved chopped parsley with the couscous and spoon it over the sauce. Sprinkle the cheese on top – it will stop the couscous from crisping up too much – then drizzle over the olive oil. Bake the crumble in the preheated oven for about 10 minutes until everything is piping hot. Serve with some seasonal green vegetables.

388 calories per serving

CHICKEN AND PRAWN LAKSA

It might look like a lot to do here but the ingredients for the paste can be chopped roughly, as they will be blitzed, and the cooking is brief. You can use shop-bought laksa paste if you prefer, but the flavour won't be quite as punchy.

SERVES 4

1 tsp vegetable or coconut oil

500g skinless, boneless chicken breasts or thighs, diced

400ml can of reduced-fat coconut milk

600ml hot chicken stock

1–2 tbsp fish sauce

2 Kaffir lime leaves, finely shredded

1 carrot, cut into matchsticks

100g rice vermicelli

200g Chinese greens – any sort

100g bean sprouts

300g shelled raw prawns

juice of 1 lime

fresh coriander leaves

flaked sea salt

freshly ground black pepper

Laksa paste (or use a small jar of laksa paste)

2 lemongrass stalks, white centre only, roughly chopped

3 garlic cloves, roughly chopped

2 shallots, roughly chopped

10g fresh root ginger, chopped

2 Thai chillies, roughly chopped

1 tbsp puréed galangal (optional)

1 tsp shrimp paste

1 tsp ground cumin

1 tsp ground turmeric

If you're making your own paste, put all the ingredients in a food processor with a little water to get the mixture going and blitz until fairly smooth. Set aside.

Heat the oil in a large casserole dish or a wok. When it's shimmering, add the chicken and stir-fry for a minute or so just to seal and brown it all lightly, then turn down the heat and add the laksa paste. Stir for another couple of minutes, then pour in the coconut milk and stock.

Season with a tablespoon of the fish sauce, then add the lime leaves and the carrot and leave the laksa to simmer for 5 minutes. Taste and add the rest of the fish sauce if you think it needs it.

Cook the rice vermicelli according to the packet instructions, then drain.

Shred the greens and add them to the laksa. Cook for another couple of minutes, then add the bean sprouts, prawns and noodles. Simmer for a minute until the prawns have turned pink and opaque, then add the lime juice and more salt and pepper if you think it necessary. Serve sprinkled with plenty of fresh coriander.

428 calories per serving

TURKEY KEEMA PEAS

The trad keema pea dish is made with lamb, but our turkey mince version has far fewer calories and still tastes awesome. Best to get turkey thigh mince, rather than breast which will dry out more, or if you have a friendly local butcher, you could ask for minced chicken thighs which will also work well.

Heat the oil in a large lidded saucepan. Add the onion and fry it briskly over a high heat for a couple of minutes, stirring regularly, then add the garlic and ginger. Fry and stir for another minute.

Add the coriander leaves, curry powder and mince. Stir until the mince has browned slightly and is well coated with the spices. Add the bay leaf and pour in the tomatoes and the coconut milk. Season with salt and pepper.

Bring to the boil and cover the pan again. Simmer over a medium heat for 5 minutes, then take the lid off the pan and add the peas. Bring to the boil again, stir thoroughly, then turn down the heat and leave the mixture to simmer, uncovered, for another 10 minutes until the sauce has thickened. Serve sprinkled with plenty of coriander leaves. A small portion of rice or cauliflower rice alongside is nice.

SERVES 4

1 tsp coconut or vegetable oil

1 onion, finely chopped

2 garlic cloves, finely chopped

10g fresh root ginger, grated

small bunch of coriander, stems and leaves separated, stems finely chopped

1 tbsp mild curry powder

600g turkey thigh mince

1 bay leaf

400g can of chopped tomatoes

200ml reduced-fat coconut milk

250g petits pois, defrosted

flaked sea salt

freshly ground black pepper

270 calories per serving

STICKY CHICKEN DRUMSTICKS

There's nothing like a sticky drumstick. If anything, these are even better once they've cooled down, as the flavour develops, so they make a great treat to pop in your lunch box. Otherwise, serve them with a salad or any kind of veg you like. If you have any left over, strip off the meat and pack it into a wrap.

Preheat the oven to 180°C/Fan 160°C/Gas 4. Line a baking tray with baking parchment.

Using a sharp knife, slash the drumsticks through to the bone at intervals and put them on the baking tray. Bake them in the oven for 10 minutes.

Meanwhile, mix all the glaze ingredients together and season the mixture with salt and pepper. Remove the chicken drumsticks from the oven and brush them with half the glaze. Turn the oven up to 220°C/Fan 200°C/Gas 7 and bake the chicken for another 5 minutes.

Take the chicken out of the oven again and brush over the rest of the glaze, then cook for another 5 minutes. The chicken should be dark and sticky and completely cooked through.

SERVES 4

8 chicken drumsticks, skinned

Glaze

1 tbsp soy sauce

1 tbsp apricot jam

1 large garlic clove, crushed

5g fresh root ginger, grated

1 red chilli, deseeded and very finely chopped

1 tsp Chinese five-spice

flaked sea salt

freshly ground black pepper

223 calories per serving

CAULIFLOWER PILAF

Everyone loves a pilaf but the rice makes it quite a high-calorie dish. But if you use cauliflower instead of rice you get all that lovely comforting flavour and texture with far fewer cals. We're happy putting the whole spices into our pilaf and we're used to fishing them out as we eat, but if you're worried you could wrap them in a little bit of muslin and tie it at the top.

SERVES 4

500g skinless, boneless chicken breasts or thighs

large pinch of saffron

1 large onion, sliced into thin crescents

2 garlic cloves, finely chopped

5g fresh root ginger, finely chopped

1 tbsp vegetable or coconut oil

5 cardamom pods

2 x 3cm pieces of cinnamon stick

1 tsp cumin seeds

1 tsp fennel seeds (optional)

3 cloves

2 bay leaves

250ml hot chicken stock

1 medium cauliflower (about 750g)

flaked sea salt

freshly ground black pepper

To serve

1 tbsp pistachios

½ pomegranate

small bunch of coriander or parsley

274 calories per serving

First prepare the chicken. If using thighs, trim off any fat, then slice them thinly. If using chicken breasts, cut them into 2cm chunks. Put the saffron in a bowl with a little hot water and leave it to steep.

Heat the oil in a large, lidded frying pan or a shallow casserole dish. When the pan is hot, add the chicken. Fry the chicken for a minute, stirring constantly, until the pieces have seared, then add the onion, garlic and ginger and fry for another couple of minutes. Add the whole spices and the bay leaves.

Pour the stock and the saffron with its water into the pan, then season. Stir well, scraping up any brown bits from the base of the pan. Bring the stock to the boil, then leave to simmer while you prepare the cauliflower – this should take about 5 minutes. Cut up the cauliflower and blitz to the size of coarse breadcrumbs in a food processor – use the stalks as well as the florets.

When the liquid has reduced so it just coats the base of the pan and the chicken and onion are tender, remove the chicken and most of the onion with a slotted spoon and keep them warm. Add the cauliflower to the pan and stir so it is coated with the remaining liquid and spices – it should start to turn a light ochre in patches.

Cook over a medium heat for at least 5 minutes, stirring regularly, until the cauliflower is cooked through and the remaining liquid has evaporated. The cauliflower should be fluffy. Put half the chicken and onion back into the pan and stir it through the cauliflower, then add the rest on top.

While the cauliflower is cooking, lightly crush or chop the pistachios and remove the seeds from the pomegranate. Serve the pilaf sprinkled with the pistachios, pomegranate seeds and herbs.

PORK AND BLACK BEAN STEW

This is based on feijoada, a Brazilian favourite made with sausage, fatty pork ribs or shoulder and beans. The classic dish takes a long time to cook, but our version uses leaner cuts of meat that are cooked quickly and briefly so they don't dry out. It's still really rich and tasty though. Worth getting some good free-range pork for this if you can.

SERVES 4

300g lean pork steaks or tenderloin

75g smoked back bacon

1 large onion

2 garlic cloves

2 tsp olive oil

100g kabanos sausage

2 bay leaves

1 tsp dried oregano

stems from a small bunch of coriander, finely chopped

½ tsp chilli flakes (optional)

2 x 400g cans of black beans

300ml hot chicken stock

1 tbsp red wine vinegar

flaked sea salt (optional)

freshly ground black pepper

Salsa

1 tomato, finely diced

½ red pepper, finely diced

juice of 1 lime

½ tsp ground cumin

leaves from a small bunch of coriander, roughly chopped

flaked sea salt

freshly ground black pepper

Trim the pork of any fat and cut it into thin strips. Trim the bacon of any fat and dice. Peel and slice the onion into thin crescents and finely chop the garlic.

Heat half the olive oil in a large saucepan or a casserole dish. Add the bacon and onion and fry over a high heat for 3–4 minutes, then add the garlic, pork and sausage. Cook for another minute.

Add the bay leaves, oregano and coriander stems to the pan, together with the chilli flakes, if using. Pour in the black beans – with their liquid – then rinse out the tins with the chicken stock and pour this in too. Add the vinegar and season with pepper and salt, if needed – don't add salt at this stage if your black beans were in salted water.

Bring the stew to the boil, then turn down the heat and simmer for 10 minutes. The texture should be soupy but not runny.

While the pork and beans are cooking, make the salsa. Put the diced tomato and pepper in a bowl and add the lime juice and cumin. Season with salt and pepper and add the coriander leaves. Stir to combine, then leave to sit until the stew is ready.

Serve the pork and beans in bowls, with the salsa on the side to dollop on top.

380 calories per serving

BEEF STIR-FRY

Stir-fries are the speed dieter's best friend and this one completely fills the brief for a quick, healthy, low-cal meal. It's inspired by dishes we ate on our trip to Korea a couple of years ago. Just keep your portion of noodles down and fill up on all the lovely veg.

First cook the noodles, according to the packet instructions, then drain and toss them in the sesame oil. Trim the beef of any fat and cut the meat into thin strips.

Heat the vegetable oil in a wok. Add the red pepper and carrot and stir-fry for 3 minutes over a high heat. Add the spring onions and mushrooms and cook for another 2 minutes, then add the beef, garlic and root ginger. Continue to stir-fry until the beef is seared on all sides.

Trim the greens and slice them if the leaves are large. Pour the soy sauce and rice wine vinegar into the wok and add the greens, then cook over a slightly lower heat until the greens have wilted down. Add the noodles and warm them through.

Serve at once, sprinkled with sesame seeds.

SERVES 4

100g rice noodles

½ tsp sesame oil

300g steak (sirloin, flank, bavette or rump)

1 tbsp vegetable oil

1 red pepper, deseeded and sliced into strips

1 large carrot, cut into matchsticks

4 spring onions, cut into 1cm rounds

200g shiitake mushrooms

2 garlic cloves, finely chopped

5g fresh root ginger, finely chopped

large bag of pak choi or other Asian greens

2 tbsp soy sauce

1 tsp rice wine vinegar

1 tsp sesame seeds (white or black), to serve

283 calories per serving

AMERICAN BISCUITS

In the American Deep South, biscuits are essential for mopping up your grits and gravy.
But they're not what we think of as biscuits in the UK – they're more like a kind of savoury scone
and very good. Like corn bread, biscuits are made with a raising agent, not yeast, so are
quick to do. Try these with our chicken casserole on page 149 – they make a great bit on the side.

MAKES 8

200g plain flour, plus extra
for dusting

2 tsp baking powder

¼ tsp bicarbonate of soda

½ tsp salt

25g cold butter, diced

150ml buttermilk, plus extra
for brushing

V ❄ *124 calories per biscuit*

Preheat the oven to 220°C/Fan 200°C/Gas 7.

Put the plain flour in a food processor with the baking powder, bicarbonate of soda and salt. Add the butter, then process until the mixture resembles fine breadcrumbs. Pour in the buttermilk and process briefly again – the mixture should clump together and be slightly tacky.

Turn the dough out on to a lightly floured surface and knead a few times until it's well combined and smooth. Roll the dough out to a thickness of about 1.5cm and cut out rounds with a 6cm cookie cutter. Dip the cutter in flour each time so that it doesn't stick to the dough. You should get 8 biscuits.

Arrange the biscuits on a baking tray and brush them with a little more buttermilk. Bake them in the oven for 10–12 minutes. Best served while still warm.

QUICK CORN BREAD

Corn bread is a quick bread made with bicarb and baking powder instead of yeast, and is very popular in the States as a side dish. It's often served dripping with butter, but we like it just as it is with black-eyed peas and greens (see page 119). It's a perfect way of soaking up the juices. We've suggested greasing the pan with a little spray oil, but if you want a bit of extra flavour and you're not vegetarian, use a few grams of lard or pork dripping instead. We cut this into small squares – just try not to eat too many of them!

Preheat the oven to 220°C/Fan 200°C/Gas 7. Spray a 20 x 20cm brownie tin with low-cal oil and put it in the oven to heat up.

Put the cornmeal and flour in a large bowl with the baking powder, bicarbonate of soda and salt. Whisk the eggs and buttermilk together, then add them to the dry ingredients. Add the sweetcorn and jalapeños, if using, and mix thoroughly.

Remove the tin from the oven, then as quickly as you can, spread the batter evenly over the base of the tin. The easiest way to do this is with a palette knife. Put the tin back in the oven and bake the corn bread for 15 minutes until it's well risen and deep golden-brown. Remove the corn bread from the oven and allow it to cool a little before cutting it into about 25 squares.

MAKES 25 SMALL SQUARES

low-cal oil spray
250g medium-coarse cornmeal
100g plain flour
1 tbsp baking powder
¼ tsp bicarbonate of soda
½ tsp salt
2 large eggs
284ml carton of buttermilk

Extras (optional)

200g sweetcorn
25g jalapeño slices (from a jar)

67 calories per square

SLOW, SLOW, QUICK, QUICK, SLOW

SLOW-COOKER BARLEY AND VEGETABLE STEW

SLOW-COOKER CHICKEN TAGINE

POT-ROAST BEEF

PRESSURE-COOKER RISOTTO

QUICK CHICKEN CASSEROLE

LAMB CURRY, DHANSAK STYLE

VEGETABLE DHAL

PRESSURE-COOKER TOMATO SAUCE

POACHED PEARS

CHOCOLATE MUG CAKE

SLOW-COOKER BARLEY AND VEGETABLE STEW

It may seem strange to include slow-cooker recipes in a fast food cookbook, but there is method in our madness! It's simply a case of spending that half hour of food prep in the morning, instead of in the evening. Gremolata is a cheeky little Italian number, often used to garnish slow-cooked meat dishes. It's finely chopped garlic, parsley and lemon zest and is just right for adding a tang of freshness to this stew.

SERVES 4

10g dried mushrooms (optional)

1 onion, finely chopped

1 celery stick, finely chopped

1 red pepper, finely chopped

1 large carrot, diced

200g butternut squash or sweet potato, diced

3 garlic cloves, finely chopped

a few sprigs of rosemary

1 tsp dried oregano

150g pearl barley

1 litre hot vegetable stock

shavings of Parmesan cheese or a vegetarian alternative

flaked sea salt

freshly ground black pepper

Gremolata (optional)

small bunch of parsley, finely chopped

zest of 1 lemon

2 garlic cloves, finely chopped

If using the mushrooms, soak them in a small dish of warm water for a few minutes while you prepare the vegetables.

Put the vegetables in the slow cooker with the garlic, rosemary, oregano and barley. Season with salt and pepper, then pour over the stock. Add the dried mushrooms and their soaking water.

Put the lid on the slow cooker and leave to cook on low for about 5 hours. By this point the barley should be cooked through and plump and the vegetables should be tender but still holding their shape.

To make the gremolata, mix the parsley, lemon zest and garlic together. Serve the barley stew garnished with the gremolata, if using, and some shavings of cheese.

V ❄ *241 calories per serving*

SLOW-COOKER CHICKEN TAGINE

Tagines are not usually an option for a mid-week supper, as they take ages to cook. But pop everything in your slow cooker in the morning and you'll be rewarded with the magical aromas of Morocco when you get home and a perfectly cooked meal. Yum.

SERVES 4

1 onion, thinly sliced

2 garlic cloves, finely chopped

1 tbsp ground coriander

1 tbsp ground cumin

1 tbsp ground ginger

½ tsp cinnamon

¼ tsp ground cloves

zest and juice of 1 lemon

400g can of chickpeas, drained and rinsed

8 bone-in chicken thighs, skinned

8 dried apricots

25g pitted green olives

250ml hot chicken stock

flaked sea salt

freshly ground black pepper

Put the onion and garlic in the slow cooker and add all the spices and the lemon zest. Stir to mix everything together.

Add the chickpeas, then arrange the chicken thighs on top. Slice each apricot in half through the middle to create 2 thin pieces (rather than 2 semi-circles) and add them to the slow cooker with the olives. Season with salt and pepper and pour over the chicken stock.

Put the lid on and cook on low for 8 hours. Add the lemon juice towards the end of the cooking time.

Good served with cauliflower couscous or the regular kind, sprinkled with parsley.

❄ *355 calories per serving*

POT-ROAST BEEF

Okay, this one is a little more work than the other slow-cooker recipes but it's well worth it. As we've always said, cheaper cuts of meat such as chuck and silverside have the best flavour and this is a prime example. BTW, if you don't want to make your own bouquet garni, you can use a shop-bought one.

SERVES 6

1 tbsp plain flour

1 tsp mustard powder

1 tsp mixed herbs

1.2–1.5kg beef chuck or silverside, trimmed of fat

1 tbsp olive oil

1 onion, finely diced

2 carrots, finely diced

2 celery sticks, finely diced

2 garlic cloves, finely chopped

1 tbsp tomato purée

1 tbsp anchovy paste

200ml red wine

500ml hot beef stock

bouquet garni made of a sprig of thyme, 2 sprigs of parsley and 2 bay leaves

flaked sea salt

freshly ground black pepper

❄ *367 calories per serving*

Sprinkle the plain flour over a plate and season it with salt and pepper. Add the mustard powder and herbs and mix thoroughly. Roll the beef in the flour mixture until it's completely covered, then pat off any excess.

Heat 1 teaspoon of the olive oil in a frying pan. Sear the beef on all sides – this will take at least 2–3 minutes on each side so while this is happening, prepare the vegetables and garlic.

When the beef is browned, remove it from the pan and set it aside. Put the remaining oil in the pan, add the vegetables and garlic and cook them over a high heat for several minutes until they're starting to take on some colour. Add the tomato purée and anchovy paste and stir for another minute or so to cook the purée.

Pour the red wine into the pan and allow it to bubble, scraping up any brown bits from the base of the pan. Pour the entire contents of the pan into the slow cooker and add the beef. Pour over the beef stock and tuck in the bouquet garni, then season with a little salt and pepper.

Cook at a low heat for 7–8 hours until the beef is very tender. When the meat is ready, remove it from the slow cooker. Strain the cooking liquid into a saucepan, reserving the vegetables, and boil it for a few minutes to reduce it to a thick gravy. Serve the beef in thick slices with the vegetables and gravy. Some greens make a good accompaniment.

PRESSURE-COOKER RISOTTO

Risotto is one of our favourite dishes but it usually means standing over the saucepan stirring and that's not always what you feel like after a hard day's work. The good news is that with a pressure cooker, you can have a perfect risotto in no time – and with very little stirring. If you don't have a pressure cooker, make this in the usual way, adding the stock a little at a time, but it will take more than half an hour.

Heat the olive oil and butter in the pressure cooker. Add the onion and cook it gently for 5 minutes, until it has started to soften, then add the garlic, courgette, lemon zest and rice. Continue to stir for a minute so the rice becomes well coated with the oil and butter.

Turn up the heat and pour the white wine into the pan. Allow it to bubble up for a minute or so until it has reduced, then pour in the stock. Season with salt and pepper.

Click the pressure cooker lid into place and leave it over a high heat until it comes up to pressure. Turn the heat down and leave to cook at high pressure for exactly 5 minutes, then fast release.

While the risotto is cooking, bring a kettle of water to the boil. Put the peas in a bowl and pour half the water over the peas to defrost them and pour the rest into a saucepan. Shred the greens and put them in the saucepan with the drained peas. Bring the water to the boil and cook the peas and greens for 2–3 minutes until they're cooked through but still a nice fresh green, then drain.

Put the pressure cooker over a low heat, with the lid off. Add the peas and greens to the pan together with the grated cheese. Beat until the cheese has melted and the risotto is creamy. Serve immediately.

SERVES 4

1 tsp olive oil

5g butter

1 onion, finely chopped

2 garlic cloves, finely chopped

1 large courgette, diced

1 tsp lemon zest

200g Arborio risotto rice

75ml white wine

400ml hot vegetable stock

100g frozen peas

100g chard, kale or spring greens

25g Parmesan cheese or a vegetarian alternative, grated

flaked sea salt

freshly ground black pepper

319 calories per serving

QUICK CHICKEN CASSEROLE

You can make a beautiful chicken casserole in less than half an hour in a pressure cooker, so for the impatient healthy eater, one of these bits of kit could be a welcome addition to your kitchen. We love this served with our American biscuits (see page 136) to mop up the lovely juices.

Cut the chicken thighs in half, or quarters if they're particularly large. Heat the olive oil in the pressure cooker, add the chicken thighs and cook them over a high heat for a couple of minutes or until seared all over. Remove them with a slotted spoon and set aside. Add the onion to the pan and cook for another few minutes.

Add the garlic, mushrooms and butternut squash and cook for another 2 minutes. Put the chicken back in the pressure cooker and sprinkle in the sage. Stir in the mustard and pour the white wine and chicken stock into the pan.

Season with salt and pepper, then click the lid into place and bring the cooker up to high pressure. Cook for 4 minutes at high pressure, then remove the pan from the heat and allow the pressure to drop naturally.

When the pressure has dropped, remove the lid, add the crème fraiche and simmer over a low heat until the sauce is slightly reduced. Sprinkle the casserole with parsley just before serving.

SERVES 4

500g skinless, boneless chicken thighs

1 tbsp olive oil

1 onion, thickly sliced

2 garlic cloves, finely chopped

200g button mushrooms, wiped clean

300g butternut squash, cut into chunks of about 3cm

1 tsp dried sage

1 tsp Dijon mustard

100ml white wine

100ml hot chicken stock

2 tbsp half-fat crème fraiche

2 tbsp finely chopped parsley

flaked sea salt

freshly ground black pepper

250 calories per serving

LAMB CURRY, DHANSAK STYLE

A curry like this usually needs to simmer for hours but you can make a great version in a pressure cooker. Be sure to heat the stock before you pour it in or you will slow things down. If you don't have all the spices, you can use a medium curry powder instead – about a tablespoon should do it. Nice with cauli rice instead of regular rice to keep the calories down.

SERVES 4

750g stewing lamb (leg or shoulder)

1 tbsp vegetable or coconut oil

1 onion, thickly sliced

3 garlic cloves, finely chopped

10g fresh root ginger, finely chopped

12 dried apricots

1 tbsp ground coriander

1 tsp ground cardamom

1 tsp turmeric

½ tsp ground cinnamon

½ tsp cayenne pepper

¼ tsp ground cloves

50g red lentils, rinsed

300ml hot chicken or lamb stock or water

juice of ½ lemon

fresh coriander, to serve

flaked sea salt

freshly ground black pepper

Trim any visible fat off the lamb and dice the meat into bite-sized pieces. Heat the oil in the pressure cooker. Add the lamb, onion, garlic and ginger and cook over a high heat for 2 minutes. Meanwhile, slice each apricot in half through the middle, so you end up with 2 thin pieces rather than semi-circles.

Sprinkle the spices over the lamb, then add the lentils and apricots. Pour in the hot stock and season with salt and pepper. Close the lid of the pressure cooker and cook over a high heat until it reaches pressure. Cook for 12 minutes at high pressure, then if you have time, let the pressure drop naturally – otherwise go for fast release.

When the pressure has dropped, remove the lid and stir in the lemon juice. Serve the curry sprinkled with fresh coriander.

414 calories per serving

VEGETABLE DHAL

This is not one of your dribbly dhals but a proper meal in itself, especially if served with some rice or flatbread. And we find it's even better cooked in a pressure cooker than in a regular pan. A green vegetable alongside is nice too.

SERVES 4

1 tbsp vegetable or coconut oil

1 onion, finely diced

2 garlic cloves, finely chopped

5cm fresh root ginger, grated

2 tbsp coriander stems, finely chopped

1 sweet potato, diced

1 tbsp curry powder

200g red lentils

500ml hot vegetable stock or water

400g can of chopped tomatoes

50g frozen spinach or 100g fresh spinach

flaked sea salt

freshly ground black pepper

To serve

a few green chillies, thinly sliced

a few coriander leaves, torn

lemon wedges

V ❄ *315 calories per serving*

Heat the oil in the pressure cooker and add the onion. Cook it over a medium heat for 5 minutes until it's starting to take on some colour, then add the garlic, ginger, coriander stems, sweet potato and curry powder. Stir thoroughly for a minute or so until everything is well coated with the curry powder.

Add the red lentils, then pour the hot stock or water and the tomatoes into the pan. Season with salt and pepper and stir thoroughly again. Add the spinach – if using frozen spinach you can defrost it in hot water first, if you like, but you don't have to.

Click the lid into place and bring the cooker up to high pressure. Turn down the heat and cook the dhal at high pressure for 1 minute only, then remove from the heat and leave the pressure to drop naturally. The lentils will continue to cook during this time.

When the pressure has dropped, remove the lid and stir vigorously so everything is well combined. Garnish with the chillies and coriander and serve with lemon wedges to squeeze over the top.

PRESSURE-COOKER TOMATO SAUCE

*We like to make plenty of this and stash some away in the freezer for another day.
A good tomato sauce usually needs a good hour to bubble and reduce, but you can make
one in the pressure cooker in less than half the time. Great to serve with pasta or
with some meatloaf or burgers.*

Heat the olive oil in the pressure cooker and add the onion.
Cook it over a medium to high heat for 5 minutes, stirring
regularly, until it starts to colour around the edges.

Add the garlic and cook for another minute. Turn up the heat
and pour in the white wine, then let it bubble furiously for a
couple of minutes. Strip the leaves from the basil and add the
stems to the pressure cooker, keeping the leaves aside. Sprinkle
in the oregano, then pour the tomatoes into the pan and season
with salt and black pepper.

Close the lid of the pressure cooker and bring it up to high
pressure. Cook the sauce at high pressure for 10 minutes, then
fast release. Leave the sauce to simmer, uncovered, for another
5 minutes to reduce a little. Shred the basil leaves and stir them
in at the last minute.

SERVES 4

1 tbsp olive oil

1 onion, finely diced

3 garlic cloves, finely chopped

150ml white wine

small bunch of basil

1 tsp dried oregano

2 x 400g cans of chopped tomatoes

flaked sea salt

freshly ground black pepper

---

111 calories per serving V

POACHED PEARS

Normally, poached pears take at least half hour to cook but in the pressure cooker they take six minutes. They're good to eat and make a reasonably healthy dessert, as you discard most of the sugar syrup they're cooked in. We've cut down the sugar in the syrup as much as we dare so it's best to use fairly sweet pears if you can find them. The amaretti biscuits add a lovely crunch and they're only 29 calories each.

Put the hot water and white wine in the pressure cooker with the sugar. Split the vanilla pod down the middle and add this too. Put the pan over a low heat and stir until the sugar has completely dissolved.

Put the lemon or lime juice into a large bowl and add cold water. Peel the pears, removing the cores from the base, and drop each one into the bowl of citrus water as you go – this stops the pears going brown.

When you have prepared all the pears, strain them and add them to the pressure cooker. Close the lid, bring the cooker up to high pressure, then turn down the heat and cook at high pressure for 6 minutes.

Fast release the pressure and open the lid. Remove the pears and let them cool down for a while before serving – they are best at room temperature.

Crumble the amaretti biscuits until they are the consistency of breadcrumbs. Serve the pears in individual bowls, with a little crème fraiche sprinkled with biscuit crumbs.

SERVES 6

500ml hot water

100ml white wine

100g caster sugar

1 vanilla pod

juice of ½ lemon or lime

6 ripe but firm pears

To serve

4 small amaretti biscuits

4 tbsp half-fat crème fraiche

176 calories per serving

CHOCOLATE MUG CAKE

For those moments when only cake will do, try our microwave wonders. We realise you might have to keep your lunch very low-cal if you're going to treat yourself to one of these but they're so quick and easy – and good – it could be worth it.

Put the plain flour, cocoa, espresso powder, baking powder and sugar in a bowl and whisk to remove any lumps.

Mix all the remaining ingredients, except the oil, together. Add them to the dry ingredients and stir thoroughly until smooth.

You need a mug that holds about 200ml and can go in the microwave. Spray it with low-cal oil, then pour in the cake batter.

Put the mug in the centre of your microwave and cook on high power for 1 minute only. Check to see if the cake is done – you want it to be cooked on top and slightly springy. If it's not quite ready, cook for another 15 seconds.

Delve in and eat the cake from the mug with perhaps a spoonful of half-fat crème fraiche.

SERVES 1

2 tbsp plain flour

1 tbsp cocoa

½ tsp instant espresso powder

¼ tsp baking powder

1 tbsp caster sugar

1 egg

1 tbsp low-fat yoghurt

10g butter, melted

2 tbsp milk

a few drops of vanilla extract

low-cal oil spray

half-fat crème fraiche, to serve

417 calories per cake
442 calories with a tablespoon
of half-fat crème fraiche

SPEEDY SWEETS

FAIRY CAKES

CRUNCHY OAT COOKIES

COCONUT AND CARROT MACAROONS

QUICK INDIVIDUAL CHEESECAKES

INSTANT SORBET

ICED BERRIES WITH WHITE CHOCOLATE SAUCE

GRILLED PINEAPPLE

RASPBERRY AND ORANGE SOUFFLÉS

QUICK RICE PUDDING

SWEET OMELETTE

BAKED BANANAS WITH CHOCOLATE RUM SAUCE

ZABAGLIONE

FAIRY CAKES

Cake for tea in half an hour? No problem. These little fairy cakes are lovely and light and so are fine just as they are, but we like to add the soft icing for an extra-special treat. Take one of these to work with you for that mid-afternoon snack attack.

MAKES 12

125g plain flour

1 tsp baking powder

50g butter, softened

75g caster sugar

grated zest of 1 orange

2 large eggs

2 tbsp orange juice

50ml 0% fat yoghurt

Icing

100g low-fat soft cream cheese

1 tbsp icing sugar or maple syrup

2 tbsp orange juice

1 tbsp grated orange zest

128 calories per cake

Preheat the oven to 180°C/Fan 160°C/Gas 4. Line a fairy cake tin with paper cases.

Put the flour and baking powder in a bowl and whisk to get rid of any lumps.

Put the butter, sugar and orange zest in a separate bowl and whisk or beat until light and fluffy. Add the eggs, one at a time, with a tablespoon of flour, beating lightly in between each addition. Add the rest of the flour, then beat in the orange juice and yoghurt. The mixture should have a dropping consistency.

Divide the mixture between the fairy cake cases – each should hold about a dessertspoonful. Bake the cakes in the oven for 12–15 minutes until they are well risen – they won't turn evenly brown because of the low amount of sugar so don't be tempted to overcook for colour. Put the cakes on a rack to cool while you make the icing.

Whisk together the cream cheese, icing sugar or maple syrup and orange juice until smooth. Swirl a little icing on top of each cake and sprinkle on a little orange zest.

CRUNCHY OAT COOKIES

Some shop-bought cereal bars are scarily high in calories so try these instead. At only 156 calories each, our cookies make a tasty little morsel with a cuppa. The oats fill you up and keep you going too.

MAKES ABOUT 16

100g plain flour
1 tsp baking powder
pinch of salt
200g porridge oats
75g raisins or chocolate chips
85g butter, softened
100g light brown sugar
1 egg

156 calories per cookie

Preheat the oven to 180°C/Fan 160°C/Gas 4.

Put the flour in a bowl with the baking powder and a pinch of salt. Whisk briefly to make sure there aren't any lumps, then stir in the porridge oats and the raisins or choc chips.

Put the butter and sugar in a separate bowl and whisk until very light and fluffy. Beat in the egg, then combine the butter mixture with the dry ingredients. Mix thoroughly.

Take tablespoons of the mixture, forming them into little balls about the size of a ping-pong ball and place them on a baking tray. Flatten them down a little so they aren't too thick in the middle.

Bake the cookies in the oven for 12–15 minutes until lightly coloured. Remove them from the oven and leave them to set on the baking tray for 3 minutes, before transferring them to a rack to cool.

COCONUT AND CARROT MACAROONS

These are not the trendy French macaroons, but the old-fashioned sort, like our mams used to bake. We've cut back the calories by adding carrot and less coconut so for once you can have your cake and eat it!

MAKES 12

2 egg whites at room temperature

pinch of salt

60g caster sugar

100g carrot, finely grated

100g desiccated coconut

1 tsp vanilla extract

1 tbsp cornflour or plain flour

84 calories per macaroon

Preheat the oven to 180°C/Fan 160°C/Gas 4. Line a baking tray with baking parchment or use a non-stick baking tray.

Whisk the egg whites with a pinch of salt until they form soft peaks – this should only take a couple of minutes. Add all the sugar and continue to whisk until the mixture is shiny and full of air.

Squeeze out any excess liquid from the grated carrot and add it to the egg whites. Add the coconut and the vanilla extract, sift in the flour, then stir to mix everything together thoroughly. Be gentle so you don't lose all the air.

Put heaped tablespoons of the mixture at well-spaced intervals on the baking tray – you should get 12. Bake the macaroons in the oven for 15–20 minutes until golden brown. Remove them from the baking tray and leave them on a rack to cool.

QUICK INDIVIDUAL CHEESECAKES

If we were posh, we'd probably call this a deconstructed cheesecake. We're not, but it's still the speediest of puds and fits the bill when you crave a bit of something sweet. Match this with a low-cal main dish and you can have a two-course supper for around 500 cals. The mixture of gingery biscuit crumbs with the mango and passion fruit is ace, but you could try plain biscuits and top with berries and a dash of lemon juice. Or you could use ginger biscuits. Up to you.

Put the biscuits in a plastic bag and bash them into fairly fine crumbs – or just blitz them in a food processor. You can leave a few little chunks if you like. Add the ground ginger and stir, then divide the mixture between 4 serving glasses or bowls.

Peel the mango and cut the flesh into fairly small dice. Cut the passion fruit in half and scoop out the flesh. Mix it with the mango and set aside.

Put the cream cheese or quark in a bowl and add the lime zest and juice. Mix thoroughly until smooth, then add the crème fraiche and icing sugar.

Add some of the cream cheese and lime mixture to each serving of biscuit crumbs, spreading it as evenly as you can, then top with some of the mango and passion fruit. Chill the little beauties until you are ready to serve.

SERVES 4

4 digestive biscuits
½ tsp ground ginger
1 large ripe mango
1 passion fruit
150g low-fat cream cheese or quark
zest and juice of 1 lime
150g half-fat crème fraiche
2 tbsp icing sugar

218 calories per serving

INSTANT SORBET

If you have some fruit in the freezer and you want a pud with very little effort, this is your answer – instant good karma. You can use almost any kind of fruit but those with lots of seeds might be a bit gritty. Strawberries, grapes and pitted cherries are all good and some supermarkets sell packs of frozen tropical fruits, such as pineapple, mango and papaya, which also work well.

Take the fruit out of the freezer about 20 minutes before you want to use it. The berries or pieces need to start softening around the edges without completely defrosting.

While the fruit is softening, put the caster sugar in a saucepan with 30ml of water and the lime juice. Simmer over a low heat until the sugar has dissolved, stirring regularly, then leave to cool.

Put the fruit into a blender with the syrup. Blitz until the mixture is fairly smooth, pressing it down at the sides frequently. Add the ice cubes and blitz again until the mixture is smooth and thick.

Serve immediately or decant the sorbet into a container and put it into the freezer.

SERVES 4

450g frozen fruit, such as seedless grapes, pitted cherries, strawberries

30g caster sugar

juice from 1 lime

6 large ice cubes

87 calories per serving

ICED BERRIES WITH WHITE CHOCOLATE SAUCE

Simplicity itself but highly pleasurable, this seems too naughty for words but it isn't that high in calories. The contrast between the cold, frosty berries and the hot creamy sauce is beyond delicious and will satisfy your chocolate cravings.

SERVES 4

400g mixed berries, such as strawberries, raspberries, blueberries, blackberries

White chocolate sauce
50g white chocolate
75ml single cream
1 coffee bean (optional)
1 tsp vodka (optional)

139 calories per serving

Pick over the berries and discard any damaged ones. Hull the strawberries, if using. Spread the berries out on a baking tray and put them in the freezer for 20 minutes – the berries won't freeze in this time, but they will frost nicely.

Just before you take the berries out of the freezer, make the sauce. Break the chocolate into a saucepan and pour over the cream. Add the coffee bean if you have one – it won't add a coffee flavour but it will add depth to the white chocolate. Pour in the vodka, if using.

Heat the sauce over a gently heat, stirring constantly. When the chocolate has melted, whisk the sauce vigorously for a minute or so.

Remove the berries from the freezer and put them in glass bowls, handling them as little as possible. Pour over the hot sauce and serve right away.

GRILLED PINEAPPLE

If you're really in a hurry, you can buy pineapple ready cored and cut up. Otherwise it's no trouble to peel and core it yourself and the rest of the recipe takes minutes. This is one of our favourite desserts when we're trying to shed some timber. Tropically fantastic.

SERVES 4

8 wedges of peeled and cored pineapple (about 400g)

juice of 1 lime

1 tbsp maple syrup or runny honey

1 tsp ground ginger

1 tbsp rum (optional)

4 tbsp yoghurt or half-fat crème fraiche

92 calories per serving (2 wedges)

Heat a griddle until it's very hot. This will take at least 5 minutes over a high heat. Put the wedges of pineapple in a bowl.

While the griddle is heating, whisk the lime juice with the maple syrup or honey, ground ginger and rum, if using, in a small jug. Pour this over the pineapple and mix thoroughly so all the wedges are well coated – it's best to do this with your hands.

Remove the wedges of pineapple from the bowl, draining off and reserving any excess juices, and place them on the hot griddle. Grill for 2–3 minutes on each side until the pineapple is heated through and is marked with char lines.

Serve with yoghurt or crème fraiche and pour over any reserved juices.

RASPBERRY AND ORANGE SOUFFLÉS

Lots of people are scared of soufflés but they really aren't that difficult and they are quick to make. Try your hand at these and you'll be surprised how easy they are – and posh enough to serve at a Downton Abbey dinner do. If you're feeling extra indulgent you could use a couple of tablespoons of orange liqueur instead of the orange juice.

SERVES 4

low-cal oil spray or 2g butter, melted

120g fresh raspberries

2 large eggs

35g caster sugar

1 tsp cornflour

zest of ½ orange, plus extra to garnish

2 tbsp orange juice

1 tsp icing sugar, to dust

105 calories per serving

Preheat the oven to 170°C/Fan 150°C/Gas 3½ and put a baking tray in the oven to heat up.

Spray the insides of 4 small ramekins with low-cal oil spray or brush them with a tiny amount of melted butter. Put a few raspberries in the base of each ramekin.

Separate the eggs. Whisk the egg whites in a bowl until they form stiff peaks, then add a tablespoon of the sugar and whisk again until glossy.

Whisk the egg yolks in a separate bowl with the remaining sugar, the cornflour, orange zest and orange juice. Add a tablespoon of the egg whites to the egg yolk mixture and fold it in, then fold in the rest of the egg whites. Do this as lightly as possible, but make sure the mixture is well combined – you don't want flecks of egg white running through it.

Divide the mixture between the ramekins, piling it up high, then run your finger round the rim. This will help the soufflés rise evenly.

Place the ramekins on the baking tray and cook the soufflés in the preheated oven for 10–12 minutes until they are lightly golden and well risen. Dust with icing sugar and scatter over the orange zest, then serve immediately.

QUICK RICE PUDDING

Fancy a pud for your tea? Team this with one of our soups as a first course and you've got a really comforting but still healthy meal, with a reasonable calorie total. We both remember our mams making rice pudding and leaving it to cook in a low oven for hours. In fact, you can cook a brilliant rice pud on top of the stove in half an hour. And for something really special, make this luxurious raisin sauce as well.

Put the rice in a medium saucepan and pour over the milk, single cream and vanilla extract. Bring to the boil, then immediately turn the heat down to something between a boil and a simmer.

Cook the rice, stirring very regularly, for 20–25 minutes. By the end of this time the rice should be plumped up and tender, and the liquid well reduced.

Add the sugar and stir until it has dissolved, then remove the pan from the heat. The pudding will thicken more as it cools so don't leave it too long.

While the rice is cooking, make the sauce, if serving. Put the raisins in a small saucepan with the Marsala and lemon zest. Bring to the boil and continue to boil until the Marsala has reduced by half. Add the sugar, then turn down the heat and stir until the sugar has dissolved. Simmer until the liquid has turned syrupy. Serve the sauce with the rice pudding.

SERVES 4

125g short-grain pudding rice
600ml whole milk
50ml single cream
1 tsp vanilla extract
2 tbsp light brown soft sugar

Marsala raisin sauce (optional)
50g raisins
75ml sweet Marsala wine
zest of ½ lemon
1 tbsp light brown soft sugar

266 calories per serving
341 calories per serving (with sauce)

❄

SWEET OMELETTE

Everyone knows that an omelette is the perfect quick meal, but a sweet omelette also makes a good speedy pudding – a little bit of eggstacy! You can use any fruit you like for the compote or just serve the omelette with fresh fruit and crème fraiche. This makes one big omelette to share between two, but you could also make individual ones in smaller pans. Arrowroot is a bit like cornflour and is used for thickening sauces and the like. It's available in supermarkets.

First make the compote. Put the blueberries or cherries in a saucepan with the sugar, lime zest and juice and add 2 tablespoons of water. Cook gently until the sugar has dissolved and the blueberries have softened. Mix the arrowroot with a little cold water in a small bowl and stir until you have a completely smooth paste. Add this to the blueberries and stir until the sauce has thickened. Keep the compote warm while you make the omelette. Put the grill on at its highest setting to heat up.

Break the eggs into a bowl and add the sugar. Using a hand-held electric whisk, beat the eggs and sugar until they are full of air and you can trail a ribbon across the surface – this should take 3–4 minutes.

Spray a non-stick frying pan with low-cal oil or melt the tiniest amount of butter and wipe it over the base of the pan so it is entirely covered. Tip the egg mixture into the frying pan, using a palette knife to make sure it covers the base evenly.

Cook the omelette over a medium heat for no longer than 2 minutes. To check the underside, lift up an edge – it should be just set and a very light golden brown. Be very careful when you do this, as the omelette is very delicate at this stage.

Put the pan under the hot grill and cook the omelette until the top is also set and starting to brown very lightly. This will only take a couple of minutes so watch the omelette constantly to make sure you don't overcook it.

Remove the pan from the grill and gently fold the omelette in half, then cut it down the middle. Serve with the fruit compote and a little crème fraiche.

SERVES 2

2 large eggs

2 tsp caster sugar

low-cal oil spray or 2g butter

2 dessertspoons crème fraiche, to serve

Quick fruit compote

150g blueberries or pitted black cherries (canned or jarred are fine)

2 tsp caster sugar

zest and juice of ½ lime

1 tsp arrowroot

237 calories per serving

BAKED BANANAS WITH CHOCOLATE RUM SAUCE

Well – chocolate rum sauce is not something you expect to find in a diet book, but we like to look after you all, and we do love something sweet from time to time. In fact, the sauce is made with a small amount of dark chocolate and isn't as calorific as it sounds, although it still tastes wicked!

SERVES 4

1 tsp butter

4 bananas

1 tbsp demerara sugar

1 tbsp rum

Chocolate rum sauce

50g dark chocolate

50ml milk

1 tbsp soft light brown sugar

1 tbsp rum

214 calories per serving

Preheat the oven to 200°C/Fan 180°C/Gas 6. Line a baking tray with a piece of foil that's big enough to overlap the edges of the tray slightly. Rub the foil with half the butter.

Peel the bananas and cut each one in half lengthways. Arrange the bananas on the foil and sprinkle over the sugar and rum. Take another piece of foil and rub it with the rest of the butter. Put the foil, butter-side down, over the bananas and crimp the edges of the pieces of foil together. Bake the bananas in the oven for 20 minutes.

Meanwhile, make the sauce. Break up the chocolate and put it in a saucepan with the milk, sugar and rum. Heat gently until the chocolate has melted, then whisk the sauce quite vigorously to make sure everything has combined properly. Remove the pan from the heat – the sauce will thicken slightly as it cools.

Take the bananas out of the oven and serve them on plates or in bowls. Drizzle the bananas with spoonfuls of the chocolate sauce.

ZABAGLIONE

Not a pudding for the little ones, as this tastes quite alcoholic. Great treat though and you could add some spices to make a festive Christmas dish. You need a heatproof bowl that fits nicely over a saucepan when making this.

SERVES 4

4 egg yolks

50g caster sugar

50g sweet Marsala wine

½ tsp vanilla extract

1 thinly pared strip of orange or lemon zest, plus extra to garnish

130 calories per serving

Bring a kettle of water to the boil. Half fill a saucepan with boiled water and set it over a medium heat to simmer.

Put the egg yolks, sugar, Marsala, vanilla extract and orange or lemon zest into a heatproof bowl that fits over the pan. Set the bowl over the saucepan, making sure that the bottom of the bowl isn't touching the simmering water.

Using a hand-held electric whisk, beat the contents of the bowl until they're light and fluffy and the whisk leaves a trail along the surface. This should take between 5 and 10 minutes. Take the pan off the heat and carefully remove the bowl. Take out the zest.

Divide the zabaglione between 4 small cups or serving glasses, garnish with orange or lemon zest and serve warm or cool.

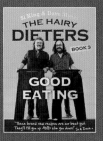

INDEX

BIG HUGS

To all you lovely Hairy people for your help in making this book, our fourth
in the Hairy Dieters series.

Catherine Phipps has done it again and helped us put together a cracking
selection of new recipes. Andrew Hayes-Watkins not only took amazing photos
of the food but also ate lots of it! What more could we ask? Anna Burges-Lumsden
and her assistants Lou Kenny and Jane Brown made all the dishes look so
tempting for the pictures so a big thumbs up to them and to Polly Webb-Wilson
for providing all the plates and pans.

We love the design – thanks to the talented Abi Hartshorne for that and to Andy
Bowden for his technical assistance. As always, thanks and love to our fabulous
publisher Amanda Harris, creative director Lucie Stericker and our editor, ideas
wrangler and good friend Jinny Johnson, all long-serving members of Team
Hairy. And we'd like to say a big thank you to Nicola Ibison – Nic, thanks for
all your help and support over the years.

We'd also like to thank everyone at James Grant Management for your work on our
behalf. Loads of love to Holly Pye, Natalie Zietcer, Eugenie Furniss, Rowan Lawton
and Sarah Hart – you're wonderful and we hugely appreciate what you do.

As well as all the above we'd like to thank the members of our Diet Club.
We're all in it together and your messages and feedback mean a lot to us.